Women in Urban Informal Sector

Women in Urban Informal Sector

D. ASHA LATHA

AKANSHA PUBLISHING HOUSE
NEW DELHI · GUWAHATI · VISAKHAPATNAM

AKANSHA PUBLISHING HOUSE
4649-B/21, Ansari Road
Daryaganj, New Delhi-110002
Phones: 23268193, 09435116718
Email: ektabooks@yahoo.com
visit us: www.akanshapublishinghouse.com

Women in Urban Informal Sector

First Published 2012

ISBN 978-81-8370-314-7

PRINTED IN INDIA

Published by Akansha Publishing House, New Delhi-110002 and printed at Harmain Offset Printers, Delhi.

CONTENTS

PREFACE

The Informal Sector has acquired great significance over the years as a source of employment and livelihood for an increasing number of people, especially women in both urban and rural areas of the developing countries. Further, small scale enterprises in the informal sector are an important and growing source of employment in many developing countries. Involvement of large number of women in the so called Informal Sector is a result of their low status in society and denial of equal opportunities in the formal sphere of employment. Participation of women in socio-economic activities assumed global significance today.

As such, an attempt has been made to study woman workers in informal sector in a fast growing city Visakhapatnam in South Asia. The informal sector activities considered for the study include petty traders, vendors, self-employed, casual labour, domestic labour, and salaried workers.

The Study attempted to analyse the determinants of work participation rates of women in the informal sector, impact of migration on income, determinants of income, savings and investment pattern and to the levels of living of women in informal sector. The study being a micro level one is of great siginificane, which in turn, helps in evolving appropriate policies and measures particularly to improve the socio-economic conditions in urban informal sector.

It is expected that this book will be immensely useful in guiding the policy makers, planners, women activitists, in the context of inclusive growth and women empowerment.

At the out set, I extend my deep sense of gratitude to my Research Directors Prof. L.K. Mohana Rao and Prof. D.S. Prasad for their guidance, constructive suggestions and sustained encouragement throughout the course of my work.

I express my thanks to Prof. S.K.V. Suryanarayana Raju, the present Head of the Department of Economics for his encouragement during the course of my work.

I acknowledge the co-operation given by Prof. R. Ramakrishna, Prof. S.Ramesh Babu (Retired) Prof. K.Venkata Reddy (Retired), Prof. (Late) N. Basakar Reddy, Prof. D. Pulla Rao, and Dr. (Smt) K. Sailaja of the Department of Applied Economics.

I am thankful to Prof. K. Sreerammurthy Pricipal of College of Arts and Commerce, Andhra University for his valuable suggestions.

I also acknowledge the kind help received from Prof. D. Harinaryana, presently Pro-Vice Chancellor, Gitam University and Prof. K. Ravi Babu (Retired) of the Department of Economics Andhra University.

I am extremely thankful to Sri K. Raghurama Prasad, Librarian (retired) School of Economics and Sri M.Venkata Rao for their help during the course of this study.

I convey my thanks to Dr. D. Narayana Rao, Dr. Jayaseela Prakash, Dr. Geetha Mohan, Ms. K Padamaja and other co-scholars of the School of Economics for their Cooperation during my research work.

I cannot forget the cooperation and help extended by the respondents engaged in various informal activities in Visakhapatnam city during the course of my study especially during field-work.

Last, but not least, I acknowledge my deep sense of gratitude towards my parents Sri. D. Apparao Garu and Smt. D. Ambujakshi, and my brother Mr. D. Shivaji, without whose continuous cooperation and moral support, this work could not see the light of the day.

I am extremely thankful to M/s Akanksha Publishing House for bringing out the book neatly.

—*D. Asha Latha*

1

INTRODUCTION

During the past two decades, based on the neo-classical framework, economic development was conceived largely in terms of attainment of higher growth rates of Gross National Product (GNP). Even if economic growth was not the solution to all social problems, policy-makers and international advisers believed that economic progress should be the single most important national objective of a developing country.[1]

However, this logic has been questioned by many economists during the past decades of the 20th century. Their arguments were based on the experience of many developing countries where poverty, inequality and other social problems have increased with economic growth. As a result, there has been a dramatic shift in the prevailing theory and practice of economic development in recent years. Inspired by Myrdal's[2] criticism of development theory, a clamour was raised by a large number of economists and policy-makers for the dethronement of the GNP and the elevation of direct attack on widespread absolute poverty, increasing income inequalities and wide spread unemployment as the objective of developmental policy. In short, economic development was redefined in terms of reduction or elimination of poverty, inequality, and unemployment.[3] Central to this new direction is the focus on 'basic needs' of the population as a fundamental objective of development in the developing countries[4]. In this regard, employment, i.e. the opportunity to participate in a socially and economically rewarding job, is considered as the most important basic need in any developing world. The desire to achieve increased level of living to population after the World

War II, across all regions, particularly in developing countries, aroused interest in development. As such, economic development has much to do with human endowments, social attitudes, political conditions, and historical accidents[5]. Development should, therefore, be perceived as a multi-dimensional process involving the reorganisation and reorientation of the entire economic and social systems.

In any developing country, like India, economic growth has been, "epitomised" in large-scale modern industries, and the like. As per Goswami[6] the concept of economic growth becomes relevant more to the growth of physical and material aspects of the paraphernalia of infrastructure than to the growth of man who despite his being the real agent behind the real growth is usually relegated to the second place in the priority fixation. Development, therefore, requires that the center of gravity must continually shift towards industry through the continuous reallocation of labour from agriculture to the industry. The related criterion of "success" in the development effort is, thus, a rate of industrial labour absorption which is quite sufficient to permit the economy to escape from the ever-threatening "Malthusian Trap"[7]. Whatever may be the reason, economic development has failed to generate adequate employment and income opportunities, notably in the modern sector which received the bulk of the resources to cope up with the problem of explosion of labourforce which does not have any employable skills.

Urban Informal Sector

The informal sector has acquired great significance over the years as a source of employment and livelihood for an increasing number of people, especially women, in both urban and rural areas of any developing world. It has particularly become a key mechanism for distributing goods and services to the urban poor. According to the ILO, the informal sector is made up of very small-scale units producing and distributing goods and services owned and operated by largely independent, self-employed producers employing mostly family labour or a few hired workers and apprentices. Informal sector enterprises, thus, are extremely diverse and are to be found in large numbers in all the main economic sectors, mostly in trade and services and also in manufacturing, construction, transport, etc. They operate with very little capital, and utilise a low level of technology and skills. Employment in these enterprises is highly unstable and incomes are generally very low and also irregular.

Women Work Participation

The involvement of large numbers of women in the so-called 'informal sector' is a result of their low status in society and denial of equal opportunities in the formal sphere of employment. Women's low status is evident from their roles both at home and at the workplace. Within the formal sector, for example, women have fewer employment opportunities, lower wages, and less job security than men do have. Moreover, women also occupy multiple roles. Many urban women, for example, work a full day either in wage employment or in the informal sector and work for long hours in domestic chores. Women and girls who leave rural areas in search of opportunities elsewhere tend to find employment in the least paid, least skilled jobs, such as domestic work, which often offer little legal protection. Nowadays, small-scale enterprises in the informal sector are an important and growing source of employment in many developing countries.

Participation of women in socio-economic activities is a global issue. Women play a very crucial part in various socio-economic activities and have now become an integral part of the global market. Female subordination has been an essential feature of human life in all contemporary societies, although with a varying degree. Women constitute about one-half of the population in India, one-third of workforce and are vital and productive workers in the national economy. The poorer the family, the greater is its dependence on women's economic productivity. Thus, enhancing women's economic productivity now is an important strategy for improving the welfare of Indian households, mostly in the informal sector. Further, women's earning have a positive correlation with children's health, nutrition levels and education. Studies have shown that Indian women contribute a much larger share of their earnings to the basic family maintenance than what the men do.

The informal sector dominated by women's economic tasks can be classified into three following categories:

(a) an entrepreneur, a self- employed worker or a wage-earner -employee producing goods and services for the market,

(b) a participant, in return for a share in the living, in the family production activities, whose products are, at least partially, meant for the market, and

(c) a contributor to the family's real income by processing some goods which are available freely in order to supplement or replace its market purchases.

Four factors generally prevail women to join the work force, namely:

(i) The inadequate income of the principal earner, which forces women to work and to supplement the income,

(ii) Mishaps, such as incapacity of the bread earner,

(iii) Death of the bread earner and

(iv) To uplift the standard of living.

Female labour participation rate in India has been much lower than in other countries. Due to awareness in women and effects of women's liberation movement etc., the female work participation rate has increased recently.

Table 1.1: Area-wise Female Work Participation Rate in India

Year	*Rural*	*Urban*
1981	23.06	8.31
1991	27.90	9.34
2001(census total)	30.98	11.55
NSS(1991-2000)	29.90	13.90

Source: 1) Census of India, 1991.

2) Computed by authoress from National Family Health Survey (NFHS) and Census estimates.

It is clear from Table 1.1 that female work participation rate in both rural and urban areas show an upward trend during 1981 and 2001. The percentage of female work participation rate in urban areas has increased from 8.31 in 1981 to 13.90 in 2000.

The Problem

One of the most determining features of development in the third world is the unprecedented growth in population and labour-force notably in large cities. In a short span, the urban population has been tripled. Concentration of investment and income in the urban/modern sector of these developing countries has attracted labour force to these centers resulting in a phenomenal increase in urban population and labour-force. In this context, on the basis of the developed experience of western countries, Lewis,[8] and Fei and Ranis[9] have advanced two-sector models for the development of labour-force in the over- populated developing countries. According to them surplus labour from the agricultural sector would be gradually absorbed in the dynamic urban economy as industrial sector expands. However, contrary to this hypothesis, employment opportunities in the modern industrial sector have failed to keep the pace with the growth of urban labourforce. The wage earning employment was found to be lagging behind rapid growth of output due to the existence of peculiar structural conditions in these developing countries. Firstly, rural sector failed to absorb the workforce.[10] Secondly, the labour absorption capacity of the modern urban sector has been more sluggish than was once assumed.[11]

Process of urbanisation has contributed to mass urban unemployment, underemployment, and extreme poverty in the urban areas of the third world. It is also intriguing to note the persistence of rural- urban migration, despite severe urban unemployment in large metropolitan areas of these developing countries.[12] As a consequence of massive rural to urban migration, the rapid growth of large cities in many of the developing countries has brought out an urban crisis of unprecedented dimensions, a crisis of inadequate urban infrastructure and housing of political and social organisation, and of employment which is most apparent in the metropolitan areas of these countries.[13] This 'premature urbanisation' or 'urbanisation without industrialisation'[14] which failed to create adequate productive employment opportunities to the rapidly growing urban labour-force resulted in a dual labour market in an urban economy. On the one hand, there is the formal sector, in which organised economic activities are concentrated and on the other the informal sector, consisting of workers who as a rule are not employed by organised enterprises and correspond in fact to the 'surplus' labourforce.[15]

They latter constitutes the residual labour market of the last resort in which persons enter as self-employed, low-income producers of marginal goods and services for lack of any other means of earning a livelihood.[16] Thus, based on the dualistic tendencies of an urban economy, urban labour market has been classified into two sub-sectors the 'formal' or 'modern' or 'organised' sector which is highly productive and is characterised by superior earnings, and the second, informal' or 'traditional', or 'unorganised' sector which generally forms the residue. Informal sector as a categorisation of unorganised activities, particularly in the urban areas of the developing economy, has gained importance in research and policy on employment, urbanisation, and development during the last decade[17]. Though the informal sector concept was first used by Keith Hart[18], it has started gaining considerable importance in the literature on development policy in general and employment policy in particular with its adoption by the ILO's Employment Report on Kenya.[19] Recognising the limited scope for employment growth in the formal sector, the ILO have launched a series of research studies in selected developing countries which not only focused light on the nature and size of the informal sector in the urban areas, but also identified several problem areas and provided estimates of the potential for employment promotion and income generation.

So far, a considerable number of studies have been undertaken in India and abroad for analysing the socio-economic characteristics, income, and employment levels in the informal sector of rural areas, but not much light has been thrown on the urban informal sector. In addition, most of the studies on urban informal sector have been concentrated on the unorganised production units and those, which do not come under the purview of the definition of a factory as given by the Indian Factories Act 1948. As a result of the liberalisation of the Indian economy and the mechanisation of agriculture, most of the rural poor are forced to migrate to the nearby urban areas for their livelihood and the urban industrial sector is not in a position to absorb this unskilled labour force. Consequently, these unskilled labour forces looked to informal sector for its livelihood. Since, the earnings of these unskilled migrated families are very meagre even for fulfilling their basic needs, the women in these families are also forced to engage themselves in some economic activities like domestic labourers (maid-servants), fruit vending, vegetable vending, fish vending, petty trading, casual labour, sales women etc., which are part of the informal sector. Unfortunately, studies undertaken to analyse the problems and levels of income, unemployment, and savings of women in urban informal sector are few and the policy makers need more studies on these aspects. Most of the scholars also emphasised the rationale of studying the problems of women in urban informal sector in developing economies like India.

As far as the State of Andhra Pradesh is concerned, there is a dearth of studies on informal sector. The State's agricultural sector is not in a position to provide enough employment opportunities for the rural poor, while the industrial sector is not in a position to absorb this unskilled Labourforce, who do not have any employable skills. As an industrially developing city in Andhra Pradesh, Visakhapatnam has a large chunk of labourforce that migrated from the neighbouring areas. It did not receive due attention of scholars. Except the study conducted by Prof. K.V. Ramana and Dr. K.S. Krishna[20] and Prof (Mrs). Tara Kumari[21], there is a dearth of studies on labourforce, especially women labourforce in urban informal sector of Visakhapatnam City. To fill this gap, this study has been undertaken with the following objectives:

Objectives of the Study:

The objectives of the study are-

(a) To analyse the determinants of work participation rates of women in the informal sector

(b) to examine the impact of migration on income

(c) to analyse the determinants of income savings and investment pattern and

(d) to analyse the level of living of women in informal sector.

Methodology

To achieve the above objectives, data were collected from a sample of 300 women respondents working in informal sector of Visakhapatnam City. In the first stage important occupations in the informal sector in Visakhapatnam are listed out, which are petty traders, vendors, self-employed (tailors), casual labour, domestic labour (maid servants) and salaried workers, etc. as they constitute important occupation for women. A pre-designed schedule on the aspects under study was prepared. Based on the observations on testing the schedule, the final schedule was revised and canvassed among the selected 300 woman respondents. The technique used for data collection was stratified random sampling method. The entire area is divided into developed and less developed ones and further subdivided into market areas and residential areas, whereas for vegetables vendors and fruit vendors data were collected from markets and Rythu Bazaars. Schedule was designed to collect detailed information from these women working in the informal sector. The present study has been carried out in a systematic way. A brief description of the universe, selection of sample, tools of data collection, preparation of the schedule, tools of data analysis and design of study are presented in the foregoing pages. The reference year of the study is 2006 and data have been collected from the sample respondents during March-May, 2006.

Sources of Data

The data were collected from a sample of 300 women respondents working in the informal sector of the city. In the first stage, important occupations in the informal sector in the city were listed out. From which petty traders, vendors, self-employed, casual labour, domestic labour and salaried workers were selected as they constitute important occupations for women. The work is based on both primary as well as secondary data. The primary data were collected from the women respondents. Household data relating to women workers are obtained through canvassing the household schedules. Data include:

1. Workers' particulars about sex, age, marital status, educational status, main occupation, subsidiary occupation etc.
2. Workers' status particulars such as self-employed, wage earners number of days worked and nature of job.
3. Employment and working conditions of workers and hours of work.
4. Facilities available in the household, sources of income, consumption expenditure on food and non-food items.
5. In-migration particulars the reasons for out-migration etc.

Secondary data relating to population, labour-force, employment are obtained from the Censuses of India for 1961, 1971, 1981, 1991, and 2001. Information regarding the occupational distribution of workers is obtained from the District Hand Book.

Selection of the Sample

As mentioned in the methodology, the technique used for data collection has been the stratified random sampling method. The entire area is divided into developed and less developed ones and further subdivided into market areas and residential areas whereas for vegetable vendors and fruit vendors data were colleted from markets and Rythu bazars.

Tools of Data Analysis

The data are processed and tabulated according to the requirements of the different aspects of the study. Simple statistical tools like percentage shares etc. are used. In addition, regression analysis is also used to analyse the data. The basic form of the Model used in the study is as follows:-

$$Y = a_0 + a_1X_1 + a_2X_1^2 + a_3X_2 + a_4X_3 + a_5D_1 + a_6D_2 + \mu,$$

Where

Y = Participation rate (Proportion of woman workers in the total number of workers in the working age group)

X_1 = Monthly per capita income in Rupees

X_2 = Sex Ratio (Number of females per 1000 males in age group 15-59)

X_3 = Dependency Ratio (Number of children less than five years of age per female in the age group 15-59)

D_1 = 1, if belongs to forward caste
= 0, otherwise

D_2 = 1, if belongs to backward caste
= 0, otherwise

m = Error term or Disturbance term

a_0, a_1, a_2 ... a_6 are regression coefficients to be estimated.

Further, the sample households have been stratified by sectors and type of jobs to investigate into the possibility of differential returns to human capital variables.

The specific variables used in the equation are:

$$\ln(Y) = b_0 + b_1X_1 + b_2X_2 + b_3X_3 + b_4X_4 + b_5X_5 + \text{m}$$

Where

Y = Per capita monthly income in Rs.

X_1 = Education variable

X_2 = Experience (No. of years in this activity)

X_3 = Productivity

X_4 = Social background

X_5 = Employment characteristics,(Sectoral Dimensions)

m = Error term or Disturbance term

b_0, b_1, b_2..., regression coefficients to be estimated.

In addition to the above-mentioned techniques, certain case studies of the respondents engaged in different activities are also presented. This enables a detailed description of the respondents' perceptions about the informal sector activity in which she engaged, the problems encountered and the measures taken by her to resolve these, etc. Further, this analysis may also help the policy makers to initiate appropriate measures for strengthening the informal sector activities.

Scope of the Study

The study is confined to the city of Visakhapatnam, which is a fast growing industrial city in the State. It presents itself as an interesting case, as its economic structure is rapidly changing for the last two decades. In the last decade alone large number of ancillary industries were established. In-migration, both from rural and urban areas has increased, resulting in a phenomenal rise in slum population in the city. The city has now been upgraded to Greater Visakhapatnam Municipal Corporation (GVMC). The study is based on the data of the women workers in the informal sector. The representative informal sector activities considered for the study include six categories of petty traders, vendors, self-employed, casual labour, domestic labour, salaried workers, and vendors were sub-divided into (i) vegetable vendors, (ii) fruit vendors, and (iii) fish vendors. The major observations and findings of the study may provide an insight into the processes, which affect and determine the economic plight of women workers in the informal sector.

Limitations of the Study and Reliability

The present study is conducted basing on both primary and secondary data. Primary data may not be free from limitations. As such, pre-testing of the household schedules was undertaken. The information relating to income was collected after data on levels of consumption were collected to get reliable information on income. A large number of respondents were either hesitatant or reluctant to give information regarding their incomes, thinking that such information may prevent them to get title deeds to their dwellings. However, all such limitations were rectified with the appropriate explanations provided at the time of data collection. In view of the possible limitations found in the pre - testing of household schedules, due care was taken to obtain the data objectively with the cooperation of other family members. Due to financial and time constraints the other occupations were not studied.

Presentation of the Study

The present study is organised in nine chapters. First chapter deals with Introduction. A review of earlier studies relating to women in informal sector is presented in the second chapter. The third chapter is devoted to present a profile of Visakhapatnam city. The fourth chapter deals with socio-economic characteristics of the sample households. Chapter five focuses its attention on migration. Chapter six studies the levels of income and savings, and the consumption pattern of the sample households. Chapter seven relates to regression analysis of the households. Chapter eight throws light on some selected case studies. A brief summary of the findings of the study, conclusions drawn and appropriate suggestions are offered in the last chapter.

NOTES

1. Hirshman, Charles, (1982): "Unemployment Among Urban Youth in Peninsular Malasia', 1970: A Multivariate Analysis of Individual and Structural Effects". *Economic Development and Cultural Change*. Vol. 30 No.2 Jan, p.391.
2. Myrdal, Gunnar, (1968): *Asian Drama*. Pantheon Book. Newyork.
3. Todaro, Michael.P(1981): *Economic Development in the Third World*. Longman Inc. Newyork, p. 68.
4. *International Labour Organisation* (1978): Employment, Growth and Basic Needs: A One World problem. Report of the Director-General of the International Labour Office, Geneva.

5. Nurkse, Ragnar, *Problems of Capital Formation in Under Developed Countries.*
6. Goswami, M.P. (1991): Neglect of Human Resource Development. *Indian Journal of Labour Economic*, Vol. 34, No.3
7. Kurien (1992): *Economy, Society, and Development*, p. 71.
8. Lewis, W.A. (1954): "Economic Development with unlimited Supplies of Labour". *Manchester School of Economic and Social Studies*. Vol. 22, May. pp.139-191.
9. Fei.H. and Ranis.G(1964): *Development of the Labour Surplus Economy: Theory and Policy-11*. Richard D Irwin Inc. Homewood
10. Economic Commission for Asia and Far East (ECAFE): Inter-relation Between population and Manpower Problems. *Asian Population Studies Series* No.7 United Nations Bangkok. (1972)
11. Hirschman, Charles: *Op cit.,* p. 393.
12. Sethuraman. S.V. (1975): "Urbanisation and Employment: A Case Study of Djakarta". *International Labour Review*. Vol. 122, No.2-3 Aug- Sept. pp. 191-205.
13. Sethuraman. S.V.(1975): "Urbanisation and Employment: A Case Study of Djakarta". *International Labour Review*. Vol. 122, No.2-3 Aug- Sept. pp. 191-205.
14. Sethuraman. S.V: *Op. cit.*
15. Souza, Paulo, R and Tokman, Victor.(1976): "The Informal Urban Sector in Latin America" *International Labour Review*. Vol.114. No.3 November – December. p. 356.
16. Lubell, Harold (1973): "Urban Development and Employment in Calcutta" *International Labour Review*. Vol 109, No 1. July – August p. 28.
17. Papola. T.S (1981): "Dissecting the Informal Sector" A Review Article on " The Informal Sector in Research theory and Practice". Jan Breman. *Economic and Political Weekly*. Vol XVI Aug.1 p. 1272.
18. Hart, Keith (1973): "Informal Income Opportunities and Urban Employment in Ghana in *Journal of Modern African Studies*. London March pp 61-89
19. International Labour Organisation (1972): Employment, Income and Equality: A Strategy for Increasing productive Employment in Kenya, Geneva.
20. Ramana, K.V. and K.S Krishna: *Urban Informal Sector:* Some Issues.
21. Kumari, Tara (1999): *Women in Urban India*. p 19.

2

REVIEW OF LITERATURE

Introduction

In this chapter, an attempt is made to review the issues elaborated in the earlier studies on informal sector. This review would be useful for identifying the issues and for formulating the methodology for the study. Eventhough study of economic development has attracted the attention of the economists right from the mercantilist school and Adam Smith down to Marx and Keynes, yet they were mainly interested in the problems, which were essentially static in nature and largely related to the Western European framework of social and cultural institutions. Karl Palanyi (1944),[1] has formulated a new methodology of allocating resources based on a significant departure from the past. Ragnar Nurske[2] pointed out that economic development has much to do with human endowments, social attitudes, political conditions, and historical accidents. Capital is necessary but not a sufficient condition of progress.

Location of industries, expansion of government administration educational institutions, commercial centers etc have to play a vital role in the urbanisation process. Due to political intervention, many developing countries have developed urban areas and large cities. (Ramana and Krishna).[3] "Better employment and income opportunities coupled with cheaper transportation and communication facilities played a significant role in attracting migrants from the rural areas."[4] In fact rapid industrialisation has been assumed to absorb surplus rural labour.

Nature of Dualism

Economic analysis of the urban areas is basically on a dichotomous mode of classification, depending primarily on a dualistic reason. As stated by J.H. Boeke (1953)[5], being a developing economy our country also has dual characteristic features in many aspects such as agriculture, industry and service sectors. Labour market has also no exemption in this regard. Not only in our country but also all over the world the labour market has dual character i.e., formal sector and informal sector. In recent years the informal sector has acquired great significance as a source of employment and livelihood for an increasing number of people, especially women, in both urban and rural areas of the developing world. The nature of co-existence of an urban market economy and the subsistence rural economy. First was explained by Boeke in his dualistic theory in a classical framework. He opines, "Dualism" is a form of disintegration which came into existence with the appearance of capitalism in pre capitalistic countries". Dualism[6] can be defined as the existence and persistence of increasing divergences between rich and poor nations and its people.

Economic Features of Dualism[7]

Several among many features of Economic Dualism are listed below:

1. The existence of the eastern or the pre-capitalistic indigenous sector of the dualistic economy has limited needs. In contrast the western capitalistic sector is the one of with unlimited wants ever increasing and being continually stimulated by demonstration effect.
2. Because of their limited needs, the eastern sector is characterised by the backward sloping supply curve of effort and risk taking, whereas the western sector is characterised by a normal upward sloping supply curve of effort.
3. The commodities in the eastern sector are not evaluated on the basic of "value in use" as in western sector but evaluated on the "prestige value".

4. Profit motive and professional trading are absent in eastern sector. Profits from speculative activities are attractive, and professional trading is conspicuous in the eastern sector.
5. The industry in the eastern sector is not investment oriented and lacks initiative, drive, discipline and organisational capabilities, which the western sector possesses.
6. The labour in the eastern sector is unorganised and unskilled, passive, silent and casual and lacks mobility, which results in wage differentials.
7. Technological progresses along the western lines are not pronounced in the eastern sector of the dualistic economies and finally
8. Lastly the eastern society is guided by "fatalism and resignation" as opposed to western society which is moulded by common sense and reason.

Mydral[8] defines "backwash" effects as all relevant adverse changes of economic expansion in a locality caused outside that locality. The effects via migration, capital movements and trade as well as the total cumulated effects resulting from the process of circular causation between all the factors, non economic as well as economic, whereas the "spread effects refer to certain centrifugal spread effects of expansionary momentum from the centres of economic expansion to other regions. Lewis considers the process of rural – urban transfer emphasizing on structural differences, Lewi, (1954)[9] and Fei and Ranis (1961, 1964)[10] consider capital accumulation as the crucial factor for the absorption of labour in the modern industrial sector. The dualistic development models emphasis transfer of surplus labour from the subsistence agricultural sector to the modern industrial sector through accelerating the rate of accumulation in the latter. According to Lewis, in subsistence sector, marginal productivity is assumed to be determined as a fixed premium over a constant subsistence wage in the traditional agricultural sector and at this wage rate, supply of labour force is perfectly elastic.

In favourable terms of trade, the modern sectors rapidly grow in a self-sustained manner through rapid accumulation caused by ploughing back of profits for further investment. In the growth process, the modern sector would draw away surplus labour from the traditional sector, until the labour surplus disappears. Leibenstein (1955),

Dobb[11] (1960) A.K. Sen[12] (1960) have supported Lewis by pointing out that the use of capital intensive techniques would generate more surplus resources which would be ploughed back into further investment and would result in greater growth of employment than is possible through labour intensive techniques. Ranis and Fei[13] described, the urban informal sector in developing countries as a low productivity backwater sponge absorbing those who cannot find productive employment in formal urban activities.

However Higgins[14] indicated four kinds of barriers to economic development. They are:

1. The dilution of incentives to save and invest
2. The limited scope of entrepreneurial spirit in under - developed areas
3. Population multiplier and
4. Backward sloping curve of effort and risk taking.

McGee (1973)[15] distinguishes between organised capitalist sector and the bazaar type peasant sector in the third world city. According to McGee "most cities in the third world can be seen as consisting of two juxtaposed systems of production - one derived from capitalist forms of production and the other form peasant system of production.

Geertz (1963)[16] attributed this to be the basis of dualism with respect to Indonesia. In such a situation increasingly a greater number of workers perform decreasingly a smaller amount of work and poverty is shared among them. The system gets involutes over time. Gradually, the urban centres become just merely large size villages and incorporate many characteristics of a peasant economy and this process is often termed as "Urban involution".

Milton Santos (1975)[17], enlarged the ILO's approach. He made a distinction between the "Upper Circuit" which is a direct consequence of technological progress represented by monopolies and the "Lower Circuit" which groups small scale activities meant almost exclusively for the poor. The terms meant that the lower circuit depends on the upper one. The latter meets the requirements of capital intensive production while, the former is created by consumption demand. Whereas in the upper circuit capital accumulation imposes work specialisation, heirarchisation and stagnation or slow growth of employment, in the lower circuit the need for a large labour force to survive is the determining factor.

Todaro (1969)[18], introduced a two sector analysis. This Model has tried to explain how more jobs in urban areas increase unemployment.

Harris and Todaro (1970)[19] further expanded this model. They assume that there are two sectors-rural and the urban or modern. The initial spurt to migration must have come from the "modern" sector in manufacturing, administrative and commercial establishments. Harris and Todaro felt that the push factors operating in rural areas were strong enough to send large supplies of labour to urban areas.

Empirical Studies on Informal Sector

In most of the literature using this concept has flowed from the studies undertaken under the auspices of international bodies such as the ILO and the World Bank. Although traditional activities and their contrast with the modern have had a long history of attention from economists, the labelling of the "informal sector" was established by the team from the Institute of Development studies Sussex who joined the ILO Mission to Kenya. It has been mush used since.[20]

Keith Hart was the first to use this concept and (1971).[21] described the informal sector as that part of the urban labour force, which falls outside the organised labour market.

Hart studied a significant aspect in urban Ghana in 1973 with regard to the existence of a variety of new income generation activities in trade and services categories in the urban areas. The study observed that most of these activities are concentrated in the "unorganised sector" and the existing data collecting machinery does not cover them. According to Hart[22], informal sector is associated with income generating activities in the unorganised and unremunerated sector. Self-employed persons are getting less than the legal minimum wage. He also questioned the traditional attitudes of treating this sector as highly unproductive and consisting of surplus labour.

The search for surplus and or cheap labour in cities switched from open unemployment to the informal sector. The informal sector in Calcutta has been defined, as the unorganised sector, which is outside the periphery of full labour enactments. Its size is quite large in most of the important urban settlements in the developing countries. It is estimated that out of the 5 million people added to the labour force of urban areas every year, only 0.5 million or 10 per cent are able to find employment in the organised sector. Deshpande and Deshpande[23] have calculated that during 1971 and 1981 the unorganised sector has grown by 4.5 per cent while the organised sector has grown by 42 per cent. It is estimated that over 60 per cent of employment in Nairobi and Kumasi, 50 per cent in Jakarta and around 45 per cent in Calcutta, Bombay, and Ahmedabad are to be found in this sector. Sethuraman (1979)[24] defined informal sector as one, which is consisting of small scale units engaged in the production and distribution of goods and services with the primary objective of generating employment and income, notwithstanding the constraints on capital, both physical and human knowhow. According to Mukhopadhyay,[25] "the boundary of the informal sector is obtained by the standard exclusion principle i.e. what does the sphere of formal sector not covered is informal sector. The sector includes petty self-employed units small units, of factory production employing seven to10 persons, shops and others establishments. Thus entire sector is a heterogeneous mix in which workers are not protected by labour legislation rules. People migrate from rural subsistence sector to the urban commercial sectors· The holding sector is in actual practice the urban traditional or unorganised sector, which absorbs the rural migrants initially in what are called the informal economic activities such as hawking, pedaling, retailing of consumer goods, working in household repairs shops, carrying head loads, pushing carts, plying manual rickshaw and so on. However, by its very nature this sector offers in secure jobs and low wages / returns. Sethuraman[26] has said, "The informal sector as its name suggests is not formal in its character. The main disadvantage of the informal sector is primarily manifest in its lack of access to the resources of all kinds, capital, finance, modern technology, and skills. The ILO-UNDP[27] Employment Mission to Kenya adopted the term informal sector to analyse the employment situation and to work out a strategy for employment generation in Kenya. "The formal activities are officially recognised and fostered by the government by providing direct access to credit, foreign exchange concession etc and on the other hand informal sector activities are largely ignored, rarely supported, often regulated and sometimes actively discouraged by government. Hart[28] used several terms "informal income generating activities", "unorganised sector", "unenmurated sector", "self-employment individuals" and "urban proletariat" in his study more or less alternatively and interchangeably. John weeks[29] attempted to make a high descriptive nature of the distinction between formal and informal sector. According to him, "the distinction is based on the organizational characteristics of exchange *vis-a-vis* the state. The nature of exchange of relationship is primarily a consequence of the economic insecurity of operations in the informal sector, which in turn is a direct consequence of the latter's limited access to the resources of all types. According to Weeks, informal sector is deprived of all the facilities like restrictions of competition and reduction in risk and uncertainly through tariff and quota protection for import substitution industries, tax rebates and holidays, low rates of interest, selective credit controls and licensing of operations, foreign technology, foreign exchange and local capital together provide disproportionally high rewards for operating in this sector. Heather and Vijay Joshi[30] While distinguishing organised and unorganised sector in Bombay under three major heads viz, markets structure, technology and relationship with the following characteristics:

> "The organised sector contains large manufacturing firms operating in oligopolistic markets sheltered from foreign competition by high tariffs and quantitative restriction, selling their products mainly to middle and upper income groups. The unorganised sector contains a very large number of small producers operating on narrow margins in highly competitive product market selling a variety of goods and activities mainly to low income groups."

Secondly, the organised firms use capital intensive, imported technology in contrast to labour-intensive indigenous technology used by unorganised sector producers. Labour productivity is much higher in the former than latter. Technology of the organised sector firms requires reutilised and formalised work conditions, while the work situation in the unorganised sector is quite informal. The organised sector firms have access to and capability to influence over the machinery of the government and therefore to official protection and benefits which are not available to the unorganised sector producers. Similar is the case with finance and credit from the organised banking sector. According to Sethuraman(1981)[31] the distinguishing feature of the informal sector enterprise is that they made their appearance, not so mush in response to investment opportunities as in the, neo-classical sense but out of necessity to create one's own employment. Thus, he said that the informal sector consists of small-scale units engaged in the production and distribution of goods and services with the primary objective of generating employment and income to them. According to Harold Lubell[32] the informal sector constitutes the residual labour market of the last resort, characterized by self-employment and low-income producers of marginal goods for lack of any other means of earning a livelihood. It is also identified as a reservoir of traditional and modern skills, which can be made productive, if effective demand is created for them.

Souze and Tokman (1976)[33] stated that this sector "comprises of all those engaged in domestic services, casual labour, the self-employed and employees of white collar, blue collar and family workers in enterprises with a total staff not more than four persons." By extension of this approach, the informal sector may be sometimes defined to include workers earning below the legal minimum wage. He also said "the contribution of the urban informal sector to urban regional income also seems quite substantial. For e.g. in Asuncion (Paraguay) San Salvador (El Salvador) and Lima (Peru)[34] this proportion was estimated to be 33, 25 and 30 per cent respectively." In Ahmedabad (India), it seems to be 28 per cent. Deepak Mazumdar'[35] has described the informal sector as the "unprotected sector".

He observed that employment in the informal sector is protected by the action of trade unions and government, while the same is denied to the informal sector labour.

Mazumdar (1973),[36] has brought out the distinction more sharply by arguing that entry into the informal labour market is unrestricted, whereas in the formal labour market it is restricted by artificially raised hiring standard norms of producers.

Bremen (1976),[37] Considering modes of production as a basis for analytical distinction between formal and informal sector describes the latter as containing a mass of the working poor, whose productivity is much lower than the modern urban sector from which most of these people are excluded.

Kenneth King (1974),[38] informality derives from their being unrecognised in government employment statistics and operating in the main out of the make shift shelters on urban waste -lands, roadsides, and forest fringes.

It is thus clear that it includes not only traditional artisans, services, and petty traders but also small units in manufacturing construction, trade and commerce, transport and services sectors engaged in the production of goods and services, which operate on a very small scale and have no formal business organisations. Thus, the various elements of the definition of the informal sector indicate a broad spectrum of heterogeneous activities of urban poor households, rising from employment, skilled and unskilled including street vendors and petty traders with low irregular incomes.

There are thus, a number of characteristics of the informal

sector, divided either on *a priori* basis or from several empirical studies on urban sector in developing countries. The meaning differs depending upon which characteristics a researcher refers to they may be grouped into eight categories as follows:

Free entry and easy to enter

"The informal sector is characterised by its fluidity and the mobility of its labour." It is the entry point to the city for immigrants who left their villages in the hope of an urban income higher than their poor agricultural income. Informal sector is also characterised as one where free entry to new enterprises exists as enterprises in this sector rely on indigenous resources.

Small size of operations

All observers agree that the informal sector consists of small establishments. The "smallness" may have differing connotations in different empirical situations. The demarcation is generally made on the basis on size of employment. "It is sometimes suggested that single workers establishments and those with only self-employed and own account workers from the core of the informal sector"[39]. From the empirical viewpoint "enumeration or registration has been considered a good base. Generally 10 workers or below is the size of employment describing informal sector"[40]. Majority of the researchers seem to hold the opinion that large cities of the third world economies operate small establishments. Smallness is usually accompanied by several other attributes, which make such enterprises disadvantaged.

Informal Structure and Family Ownership of Enterprises

Informal sector[41] enterprises obviously do not have a formally structured organisation. There is a limited functional division of labour and specialisation and most of the managerial and supervisory functions are performed by the proprietor himself. There could be extensive use of family labour. However, individual families own some of the largest enterprises in India.

Use of Indigenous and Non modern Techniques

The most important and more realistic characteristic of informal sector is labour intensive, predominantly manual, low productivity techniques of production as compared to capital intensive, highly mechanised and high productivity techniques, sometimes- foreign technology, in formal sector. Mordernisation may wipe out the informal sector to the extent that a non-modern technology may consider one of its essential characteristics. Therefore, preservation of existing technology would be quite appropriate. It also generates reasonable levels of productivity and earnings.[42]

Non Accessibility to Public Infrastructure

The informal sector might portray as having rather rough treatment in the hands of the government. It has no access to public infrastructure and state patronage like organized capital market, bank finance, foreign technology, imported raw material, protection from foreign competition, competition from formal sector, electricity and water subsidies etc.[43]

This is not because these facilities are officially denied to the informal sector but because of the meager material resources[44] and sometimes because of their inability to cope with the official procedures for obtaining them. The government tried to mitigate some of these disadvantages by giving them preferential treatment.[45] Because of limited official access to the informal sector; it is forced to enter into illegal activities, by acquiring certain inputs, with out having license, from illegal market. The bureaucratic procedures, to obtain scarce inputs, often force them into riskier black-market transaction.[46] Sometimes government forces these enterprises to move on because of overcrowding, health considerations, traffic congestions, environmental or aesthetic factor or because the land they occupy do not belong to them[47]. This is mainly because of the fact that they operate on pavements, crowded streets, and old places. Consequently, they feel insecure in these operations and are afraid of the harassment and punishment by the public authorities "The government's attempt to enforce certain regulations naturally considered by these enterprises as hostile conditions making their operations difficult[48]. Bank credit, space, electricity and water etc are examples of such services and inputs, which are not supplied on a governmental license. Yet the informal sector units are not able to avail of them adequately.

Highly Competitive and unprotected Product Market

It is also not always true that the informal sector produces goods and services of general use while the formal sector enterprises predominantly cater to the demands of high income and sophisticated sections of population and foreign markets. Nor do all informal sector enterprises operate 'in a competitive market and all formal sector enterprises operate in an oligopolistic and protected market[49]

Personal services of course are one of the important examples of an informal sector activity catering to the needs of high income groups. The informal sector generally operates in a highly competitive market and often has to sell goods and services at unfavorable terms. This is so because they are very large enough to influence the market. However, there may be few exceptions. For instance, producers of the handicraft goods in the informal sector, who operate in the market with less competition.

Unprotected Labour Market

The labour market in the informal sector is unregulated and highly competitive on the supply side with the absolute freedom of entry. While in the formal sector, it is regulated and entry is restricted based on standard hiring norms and formalised hiring procedures. The supply of labour in the informal sector consists of mostly new entrants in the labour markets. Immigrants who aspire for jobs in the formal sector but finding the opportunities for it to be limited and entry restricted, starts doing something or the other in the informal sector either as self employed, part time workers, apprentices or fulltime workers in small establishments. Thus, the labour market in the informal sector reflects absence of wage and work regulations and wide prevalence of self and casual employment. Every worker has something to do implying that entry into the labour market is merely automatic and consequently the informal sector endures the most of excess labour supply. This tends to lead to a situation of significant under employment. The workers in the informal sectors work for unusually long hours at low wages and are exposed to vicissitudes of market fluctuation and whims and fancies of their employers.[50]

Thus, the urban labour market in informal sector gives rise to insecure jobs, under employment and depressed wages.[51]

Wage Rates

In the informal sector,[52] wage rates get set not only base of labour market conditions but also to clear the market. There is enough empirical evidence that wages in the unorganised sector increased comparatively slowly than wages in the organised sector of the economy. Apparently, unorganised labour cannot have the same bargaining power *vis-a-vis* employer as organised labour and would not be enjoying the same degree of support from the government and public institutions.

All this is bound to impinge on its living and working conditions, and when compounded with other unfavourable factors, enterprises in the unorganised sector tend to keep it perpetually in low wage equilibrium.

Thus, while commenting upon the working conditions of those employed in the unorganised sector of the economy, the planners in India made the following observations. "While considerable improvement had occurred in the living and working conditions of employees in large and organised industries, owing both to state activity and trade union action, a great deal of icy way remained to be made up in respect of the workers engaged in agricultural and unorganised industries."[53] In the same manner, the national commission on labour (1969) regretted that the "government had paid inadequate attention to the unorganised workers despite the fact that they constitute a fair proportion of those who produce goods and provide services."[54] The ILO has carried out a series of studies on major cities of the Third world and estimate the size of the informal sector. As per the recommendations of the National Commission on Labour a series of studies were launched by the National Labour Bureau of the Government of India on informal sector.[55]

The first report of the Bureau considered the working and living conditions of workers in the building construction industry in Delhi. A series of studies aimed at collection of data on employment, wages, working, and living conditions were proposed at different places of the country. They include, one on jar industry at Suraj, matches and fire work industry in and around Savakasi, metalware industry in Karnataka and graphite crucible industry in Andhra Pradesh.

The growth of employment, workforce requirements, training, and education facilities etc were studied by a team of experts with reference to Visakhapatnam. The data provided by the various studies indicate that in most of the developing countries the informal sector accounts for a major share of employment. In India taking the economy as a whole, the informal sector accounted for 99 per cent of the workforce in agriculture, 78 per cent in manufacturing, 34 per cent in mining, 58 per cent in construction, 70 per cent in trade, 46 per cent in transport, and 67 per cent in service.

Women Work Participation in Informal Sector

It is a controversial issue whether women's labour participation and husband's income are inversely related. The contradiction is supposed to have been resolved by showing that when income of the family increases women prefer more leisure, which indicate that the substitution effect is greater than the negative income effect. "Women hire men as bread winners because men earn more than women in the market and men hire women to bear and rear the children as women have superior skills for this task."[56] The institutionalist look at the connection between women's non market and market work.

According to them higher entry of women in the market is associated with growing availability of women's work. Engle[57] traced the civilization. In the first, private property was unknown. In the pastoral stage, when surplus of wealth in terms of cattle, milk and meat was available the need for private property emerged. It is at this stage that there was a shift from the mother right to the father right i.e. patriarchal society. Thus Engel says that, "as wealth increased, it on the one hand gave the man a more important status in the family than woman, the over throw of the mother right was the world's historic defeat of the female sex. The man seized the reins in the house also, the women were degraded, enthralled, the slave of the man's lust, a mere instrument for breeding children. According to Patel[58] "women support a large part of the world economy by free services in home and community. Women have always been at work. Only the definitions of work and work place have not been realistic enough to include their contributions to the economy and society." "Low status, low pay, and low skills are the three pillars on which the work performance of women have rested for a long time. The author calls the sum total of this as "the non-status of women's work".

The constitution of India not only provides for equal rights and privileges for women and men but also for making special provision for women. A series of social legislations were enacted from time to time for raising the status of women in the country. On the eve of the International Women's decade, 1975-1985, a committee was set up in India to enquire into the status of women. Various studies show that women are becoming increasingly conscious of their rights and capabilities. The low status of women in large segments of Indian society cannot be overcome without opening up of opportunities of independent employment and income for them. For creating increasing awareness of the role of women in development and the need for improvement of their status, various media units under the Ministry of Information and Broadcasting have presented appealing programmers on social and economic problems and other related issues faced by women. Given the labour market conditions and the existing socio-economic environment most of the female work is in the informal unorganised sector. The labour force in the unorganised sector might be characterised by a high incidence of casual labour mostly doing intermittent jobs at extremely low wages and doing their own work at very uneconomical returns. There is a total lack of job security and social security benefits.

National Commission[59] on self-employed women has summed up the characteristics of women in informal sector as fewer and poorer opportunities to work, greater impact of unemployment, under-employment and casual nature of work, greater vulnerability because of lack of skills and education, lesser mobility, heavy responsibilities, a systematic social practice of under rating women's work, lack of access to better technologies, tools and productive assets. Largely poor women keep moving between the statuses of self employed, casual labour and unemployed. In spite of these facts, women in unorganised sector are actively involved in food production and food processing. They also participate in construction work, casual labour in the factories, work in mines, and are engaged in trade and vending in addition to the household work. Although women work for longer hours and contribute substantially to the family income, either the women themselves or the data collecting agencies and the governments as all of them do not perceive them as workers, does not recognise the multidimensional functions of women which include their productive and reproductive labour. Women quite often are the major earners for their families and this also goes unrecognised. In the past decades, there have been various forces and pressures, which have reduced women to a low and secondary place. These forces have been more dominant than those have, which have tried to push women towards growth and development. In the planning process, under the trickle down theory, it has been expected that women would equally benefit along with men. This has been belied by the actual developments. The Sixth Plan document recognized that "in spite of the development measures and the constitutional legal guarantees women have lagged behind in almost all sectors". Boserup[60] writes that the hierarchical pattern of work in the village is divided into four social groups. In the top group of high caste, women took no part in any out door activities and observe pariah. Below this top group, the women were occupied with domestic duties but never earned money for the support of the family. In third group of ordinary low caste people, women assisted their husbands in the fields and they went to the market. The fourth and the lowest social group were composed of women belonging to the poorest of low caste, who were expected to seek paid work for the support of their families.

Ramana and Krishna[61] in their study observed that within the social micro-cosm of a single Indian village, the different types of female work pattern could be clearly identified, which can represent the various parts of the world.

Working women of middle–east.

- Domestic wife who hardly contributes to family earnings a characteristic feature of many Latin American Countries.
- An active family worker who carries a large share of burden of work in the family farm a characteristic features of South East Asia.
- African type of women who cannot expect to be supported by her husband accepting whatever work she can find.

Blood and Wolfe[62] (1958) suggest that less educated women can find employment only in low status jobs, which would be inconsistent with her husband's status and might prove embarrassment both to herself and to her husband. Therefore, she will be usually satisfied with husband's income and less apt to go to work herself.

Padmini Sen Gupta[63](1960) explains that women were so far largely employed in unskilled jobs because of their backwardness, and because of rigid distinctions between the work available to women and the work reserved for men, religious and traditional conditions of women, illiteracy and cultural factors.

According to 1951 census, 94 per cent of the women workers were engaged in the informal sector of the economy of which 81.4 per cent were in agricultural occupations. The Report of the Bureau[64] (1953) after considering the economic and social status of woman workers in India in the cotton and jute textile industry, coal mining and plantation industries concludes that the status of women in India has not yet been clearly defined.

Based on the censuses of 1961 and 1971, Alice Thorner[65] said that, though not even one out of every five working people is an agricultural labour, almost half of the women who participate in work only as secondary activity, almost nine out of every ten are engaged in cultivation and the rest account for other work.

Nye and Hoffman[66] pointed out that three types of factors affect women's employment namely: 1. Those, which affect the role of a housewife and a mother. 2. Specific and general attitude of family and community. 3. Opportunities for employment. Still the decision to work might be largely influenced by the husband's attitude towards wife's work.

Raj Gopalan[67] studies the problem of role conflict in the current social situation arising out of the employment of women. He found that the women employed as nurses seem to have the effect of disqualifying them for marriage thereby bringing into conflict with their normal legitimate role in the home.

Kamal Nath's[68] study has primarily based on a comparison of work participation rate of urban women in 38 countries, describes the variation in work participation rate of urban women by status and by level of education and the distribution of workers among the principal occupational categories. It is said that the position of women in India is not unique when compared to women in other developing countries.

It still presents certain distinctive features due to traditions, backwardness, and long history of "exploitation" of women in various facets of Indian social Life.

Besides the basic points of discussion like education, religion, age, marital status, income of the informants, Chowdary[69] attempts to make a study of the problems of working women in Delhi. These areas included health of the respondents, upbringing of children, staffing household activities and their duties towards husbands, fulfilment of social obligations etc.

A study by Sengupta[70] is devoted to the understanding of the position, status, power, and role of women of Bengal dealing from the earliest day to the present time. The book tends to show that in spite of women's increasing participation in a variety of professions would be premature to believe that their emancipation is being rapidly or easily accomplished.

According to Singh[71] a quarter of the urban workers are employed in the unorganised sector as washer-women, domestic servants, and sweepers. It is important to assess not only their economic contribution but also to analyse how these women organize their time and combine the roles of wife, mother, unpaid domestic help and economic provider.

Sinha and Ranade[72] observed that women do not engage in the occupations, which involve hard and arduous physical labour. The unskilled component of construction labour in India, among whom women from an important segment, is mainly from the surplus labour force in the rural sector. Majority of them come from the category of landless agricultural labour or marginal farmers, who take up construction work to supplement their earnings from agriculture. Unemployment and under-employment leading to acute poverty of this class drive to unskilled work in construction.

Muzumdar[73] finds that a large majority of working women in India is not and never have been marginal or supplementary earners. They have always been integral and essential members of the family wanting to earn a living.

Kala Rani[74] talks about the motivations for a job. She named the motives as engagement for spare time, gross necessity, and escape from domestic chores, being used to work, have independent income, achieve own status and position, serve human being etc. She said that many of women want to make use of their education after marriage and try for jobs, where they develop interest in the job. They do not want to give up in spite of many difficulties, other women who find pleasure in earning money and want to have independent income of their own take up new occupational roles.

Murali Manohar's[75] study on women construction workers of Warangal town indicates that though the informal sector offers varied job opportunities, women prefer to undertake certain specified work. He observed that wage differentiation, turnover of equal work and the more submissive nature of women are important attractions for the employers to use women in the construction field.

When asked about the employment problems of educated women, Blumberg and Dwaraki[76] found that there is (a) Unavailability of appropriate jobs. (b) Need for special types of qualifications and (c) Case of criteria other than merit is determining appointments.

Ranade and Ramachandran's[77] study revealed that in Bombay 94 per cent relatives or husbands of employed women favored women taking up jobs. The reason for favourable disposition was found to be income- earning opportunities and improved matrimonial prospects.

Manohar[78] finds that the socio-economic situations, non-implementation of relevant laws and regulations, ineffective performance of government had a direct bearing not only on the women workers but also on the women and their status in general. Women have witnessed little change in their life style over the years and on the other hand, their conditions became more miserable. The economic conditions characterized by class structure and relations, further alienated the women from the society. The deterioration of socio economic conditions had a direct impact on their work situation.

The result of this is the alienation of women from their families, from their native places, from their jobs, from land and from human dignity.

Shervani[79] observed that the biggest motivation for work for a majority of Indian women is the economic necessity, dowry, self-expression, personal satisfaction etc. Workers face many problems like dual role on domestic front and shop floor. Working women cannot claim independent economic assets.

Gita Sen and Chinranjeevi Sen[80] studied the women's domestic work and economic activity. They feel that since women's labour force participation is mainly conditioned by economic need, by itself, labour participation significantly improves women's status in the society.

Alice Thorner and Joythi[81] analysed the urban working class women. The women workers would refer to those currently employed of engaged in occupations, which bring in income. They feel that each woman is an individual with her own distinctive personality, opinions, and hopes.

Bandyo Padhyay[82] opines that precise effects of women's participation in wage work on the family based household have received little detailed attention until recently.

This is particularly the case in many third world urban contexts where female labour force participation rates have been traditionally low until the recent emergence of opportunities for women in new gender- segregated industries, such as electronics assembly. Varghese observations on India are as follows: 1. The female work participation rate in India is not only low but also declining over the years. 2. There is high concentration (80 %) of female workers in the primary sector activities and that too mostly as agricultural labourers and unpaid family workers. 3. There is a tendency towards increasing casualisation of female employment in India. 4. Unemployment rates among women are consistently higher than that among men.

In her study of three villages in Andhra Pradesh, Miles noted that women's participation rates are grossly under reported. It was observed that women did more fieldwork than men did. In one village for which comprehensive data was collected 96 per cent of women were engaged in agricultural work while the official figure put the participation rate at 27.28 per cent, which is a great handicap in planning a development strategy of women.

Kelsell et al[83] pointed out that social class, marital status and the arrival of children could affect the career opportunities of women. On the other hand, woman by themselves appears to be relatively satisfied because of their acceptance of prevailing attitudes about the place of contemporary society. Alfred de Souza maintained that census data provide unreliable data on women largely because women interviewers have not been used in the data collection process.

The practice of obtaining information on the work done by women from a male member of the household leads to under reporting of the activity of women particularly those who are engaged in part-time work.

According to Uma Ramaswamy[84] the three major reports on women in recent times, Towards Equality (1974),

Shramashakti (1988) have assembled considerable data on the work and life styles of labouring women, their invisible contribution to the economy, state of consciousness and nascent efforts to organize them.

Saikia, et al.[85] in their study on role and status of rural women in Assam studied three-situations,i.e semi-urban, interior rural and tribal village to assess the conditions in different situations. They observed that the women are overburdened with agricultural and domestic works, which keep them busy up to fourteen hours a day. They found that discrimination of women in various aspects of life is found to be nominal. Equality of status in most spheres of life are apparent among these women.

The coming generations of women are now aspiring after activities, which give them a better status in the family and the society.

According to Ponna Vignaras,[86] the only sectors of the economy in which women remain a dominant section of the labour force are those, which demand low skills and repetitive functions and which generate low returns. As such, poor women function mainly in the informal sector, and have hitherto not been organized. Even when belonging to trade unions, they are marginalized and invisible. Along side exploitation and invisibility in economic sphere, women face an atmosphere of violence within and outside the family.

According to Errol.D' Souza,[87] two views on unemployment that have gained ascendance in the 1990s and that are increasingly dominating the policy agenda are that globalization can only worsen unemployment and that rapid technological change is resulting in jobless growth. It is these views that form the backdrop to the International Labour Office report on World Employment 1996-1997. National Policies in a global context, which terms the phenomena of globalization and technological change as the two major anxieties of the day.

K. Thakur[88] conducted a study in 1981 at Nauhatta aiming to examine the status of women in the socio-economic life of its population and the disabilities from which they suffer. The survey clearly brings out that women work for much longer hours daily and for a larger number of days in the year than men do. All of them perform double duty, unpaid household work, and paid or unpaid economic activities outside the home or within it. The ILO report argues that almost 70 per cent of workers are in service sector in industrialised countries and in developing countries, the bulk of employment is in subsistence agriculture or urban informal sector activities. As these activities are in the non-tradable sector, large chunks of workers are in activities that are not linked to the world market directly.

T.S. Papola[89] considered that labour market functions in a true competitive sense in the informal sector. He opined that in the informal sector, wage rates get set not only on the basis of labour market conditions, but also to clear the market, while wages in the formal sector establishments are rather insensitive to the labour market conditions.

Kamal Naryan Kabra[90] observes that informal sector became an arena of surviving conventional technologies and products, though in somewhat adopted forms, based on limited amounts of modern capital goods, markets, and finance and responding to local demand. However, the bulk of informal sector technology was non-patented and non- market and was generally evolved by the worker entrepreneurs themselves.

Tara Kumari[91] concluded that at the aggregate level, more than half of the women workers are illiterate and the work participation rate is 45.67 per cent. In addition, 61.78 per cent constitute migrants. She also said that at the aggregate level, education inversely influences income and women contribute 43.12 per cent to the family income.

P.K. Viswanathan[92] in their paper discusses the dynamics of the labour market in the context of the structural changes in the rubber small-holding sector.

Ineffective unionisation and collective bargaining in a State known for unorganised labour movements appear to be rooted in the social antecedents of the trappers and heir rest while peasant hood status rather than ideological mooring.

Joythi Gupta[93] in her paper has studied about brick kilns operations in northern India. These kilns operate in a largely unregulated manner in the informal sector and remain outside the purview of work place laws, with workers bound to contractors and owners by system of advance payments. Several committees have made recommendations to improve working conditions, but few of them have been implemented.

He intends that main reason for migration is the search for a regular job. The problem is not due to non-availability of skilled labour but due to poor marketability of available notional skills.

Supriya Roy Chowhury[95] analysed the critical perspectives of globalization on urban poverty and unorganised labour and acknowledge the need for mitigating the in egalitarian impact of globilasation on disadvantaged. However, scant attention has been paid to the fact that today the political leverage of the traditional protagonist of welfare the welfare state, social democratic parities and trade unions has been eroded. As such, the discourse on welfare and social security is unanchored in any kind of politics. This paper looks at the activities of the National Centre for Labour. Its relationship to traditional trade unions and leftist parties frames the discussion of the limits of the effectiveness of new unions in empowering the poor.

Sudarshan and Unni's study on measuring the informal economy and Unni and Rani's study on employment and income in the informal economy taken together, provide a comprehensive account of the dimensions of this sector, in terms of employment potentiality, scale of operations and the range of efforts and institutions that have attempted to make the sector visible.

Keshab Das[96] provides a fascinating illustration of the nature and depth of disjunction between the official portrayal of the dimensions of the industry and what another's survey has been able to unravel by capturing the various layers of functioning of the industry.

Thus, the review of studies on women workers brings the following to light:

1. Developing countries are agriculture-oriented economics. Still a large section of the population is dependent on it of which women form a large segment.
2. It is only from 1970's and 1980's that efforts have been initiated to enquire into the life conditions of women, be it in agriculture, industry, formal and informal sectors.
3. The exact nature and extent of involvement of women varies, widely across different cultures and at different stages of development.
4. Though it was believed that development automatically improved women's status, this belief has been belied by the research studies.
5. The demographic and economic factors influenced the work pattern of women.
6. Technological advancement has displaced women from their traditional activities.
7. Discrimination against women in the urban economy constitutes a pernicious form of inequality. Irrespective of the differing rates of work participation of women between developed countries there is a general agreement that women are subjected to labour market discrimination and are segregated to low paying and low status jobs.
8. Even school going girls participated in the entire household and other activities in varying degree.
9. Women have to do a large part of their domestic duties before going to work and after returning home from work outside.
10. Surveys also reveal that even when women earned 50 per cent or more of the family income, at least one third were not allowed to manage the family Funds. It was also observed that the greater a woman's contribution to the family income, the greater was her responsibility for household task.
11. Quite a significant number of the women workers are

engaged in trade activities, self- employment, and construction work..

NOTES

1. Palanyi, K (1944): *The Great Transformation,* Boston Zeacon, Press, pp.12.
2. Nurkse Ragnar: *Problems of Capital Formation in Under Developed Countries,* p.12.
3. Ramana and Krishna: *Urban Informal Sector: Some Issues*
4. Kumari, Tara (1999): *Women in Urban India.* p. 19.
5 Boeke, J.H. (1953).: *Economic and Economic Policies of Dual Societies*
6. Mehta, Meera (1985), Urban Informal Sector: Concepts Indian Evidence and Policy Implication, *Economic and Political Weekly.* Vol.,XX, No.8 February.
7. Boeke, J.H(1953), *Economic Dualism - Textbook of Economic Development* Edited by Suman. K. Mukarjee, Orient Long Man, p. 117.
8. Mydral ,G.(1957), *Economic Theory and Under Developed Region.* p. 118.
9. Lewis. W.A: *Economic Development with unlimited Supplies of Labour,* The Manchester School of Economics and Social Studies, Vol XXII, May 1952, pp. 139 to 196.
10. Ranis, G and Fei, J.C.H (1961), *The Theory of Economic Development, Asian Economic Review,* September, pp.33-65.
11. Dobb. M.M. (1960): Some Thoughts on Capital Intensity, *Review of Economic Studies* Vol. XXIII, Black Well oxford 1975.
12. Sen A.K. (1960): *Choice of Techniques Employment Technology.*
13. Ranis. G. and Fey, J.C.H (1964).: *Development of the Labour Surplus Economic Theory and Policy*: Homewood, pp.3.
14. Higgins: Dualistic Theory of Under Developed Countries. *Economic Development and Cultural Change,* 1956, pp.99 to115.
15. McGee, (1973) : Peasant in the Cities, *A paradox, A most indigenous Paradox. Human Organisation,* Washington, pp. 138.
16. Geertze Clifford (1963): "Peddlers and princes", *Social Change and Economic Mordernisation in Indonesian Towns,* Chicago, and London.

17. Santos Milton (1975), *The Shared Spare of Two Circuits of Urban Economy and their Spatial Repercussions*, London.
18. Todaro (1969): *A Model of Labour Migration and Urban Development in Less Developed Countries.*
19. Harris R.J, and Todaro P. (1970),: "Migration Unemployment and Development", *American Economic Review*, pp.126-142.
20. International Labour Office Employment Incomes and Equality: A Strategy for increasing Productive Employment in Kenya" Geneva ILO 1972.
21 Hart J.K.(1971), "Informal Income Opportunities", *Conference on Urban Unemployment in Africa at Institute of Development Studies*. University of Sussex. September.
22. *Ibid.*
23. Desh Pande and Desh Pande (1985): Census of 1981 and the structure of Employment, *Economic and Political Weekly*, pp. 20 to 22, 969 to 973.
24. Sethuraman, S.V. (1979): Some Policy Implications,Informal Sector in Developing Countries, *Social Action,* pp.196.
25. Mukhopadhyay Ishita (1994): Urban Informal Sector and Communal Violence. A Case Study of 1992 Riots in Calcutta, *Economic and Political Weekly*. August 1994.pp. 22.
26. Sethuraman, S.V. (1977): The Urban Informal Sector in Africa. *International Labour Review*.
27. ILO: Employment, Income and Equality, A Strategy for Increasing Productive Employment in Kenya. Geneva –1972.
28. Keith, Hart (1973): Informal Income Opportunities and Urban Employment in *Ghana Journal of Modern African Studies* (London). pp. 61-89.
29. Weeks. John (1975): "Politics for expanding in Informal Urban Sector of Developing" *Economic Review in International Labour Review*. Vol, III. No. 1 January, pp.2&3.
30. Heather and Joshi Vijay (1976): *Surplus Labour and city: A study in Bombay*, Asia Publishing House, pp.197.
31 Sethuraman, S.V. (1981): The Urban Informal Sector in Developing Countries, Employment, *Poverty and Environment*, ILO Geneva. p.11.
32. Harold, Lubel (1973), Under Development and Employment in Calcutta, *International Labour Review*, Vol. XIX, No. 1, July pp. 28.

33. Souza and Tokman(1976): The Informal Urban Sector in Latin America, *International Labour Review*, Vol. 114. No. 3, pp. 356-357.
34. Papola, T.S (1978): *The Informal Sector in Urban Economy – A study in Ahmedabad*, Check Grow, p.74.
35. Majumdar. D.(1975): Urban Informal Sector – *World Bank Staff Working Paper No 211*.
36. Majumdar, D.(1973): Labour Supplies in early Industrialization in the case of Bombay Textile Industries, *Economic History Review*, p. 11.
37. Bremen, J. (1976): "A Dualistic Labour Economy", *Economics and Political Weekly*, p. 187.
38. King, Kenneth (1974): Kenya's Informal Machine Makers: A Study of Small Scale Industries in Kenya's Employment Artisan Society, *World Development*, April-March, p. 30.
39. Hart, K. (1973) : Informal Income Opportunities and Urban Employment in Ghana, *Journal of Modern African Studies*, (London) March, p. 66.
40. Papola, T.S. (1981): *Urban Informal Sector in a Developing Economy*, Vikas Publishing House, New Delhi, p. 13.
41. Papola, T.S. (1980): Informal Sector, Concept and Policy, *Economic and Political Weekly*, May, p. 821.
42. Sethuraman, S.V.: *International Labour Review*, November-December 1977.
43. Sethuraman S.V(1977),.: "The Urban Informal Sector in Africa", *International Labour Review*, November-December. Vol., XVI No.3.
44. In India as also Pointed by *John Weeks*
45. Papola T.S.(1978): Small Scale Industries in Uttar Pradesh GIDS, Occasional Paper No, 2 -*Geri Institute of Development Studies*, Lucknow, (MEMEO)
46. Joshi and Joshi,(1980): Informal Urban Economy and the Boundaries in *Economic and Political Weekly*, Vol., XXIX. March
47. Sethuraman, S.V: *Op.cit*, p. 345.
48. Sethuraman, S.V.: Social Action, *Op. cit.*, p. 198.
49. The Features of Product Market have been highlighted as important distinguishing Characteristics of the two sectors by Joshi and Joshi (*Op.cit.*, p.45) and *John Weeks*.
50. Mazumdar D. *Notes on the Informal Sector, op.cit.*

51. Papola, T. S: *Op cit.* Page, No19
52. Papola T.S.: Wage Determination in the Unorganized Sector in Urban Areas, *A frame work for Analysis*, Gujarat Economic Reference Papers-Gujarat Economic Association Ahmedabad, the Informal sector.
53. Kalpagam.U(1981): Labour in Small Industry, A Case study of Exports Garments *Economic and Political Weekly,* pp.28.
54. National Commission on Labour 1969.
55. Studies Launched by labour Bureau of Government of India on Informal Sector
56. Gary, Backers, *A Theory of Marriage in New Home Economics,* George Allen and Unwin Limited 1952.
57. Engel's: The Condition of the working class in Englandin 1844, London.
58. Ahooja, Patel (1982): In her keynote Address on another Development with Women, Dhaka.
59. National Commission on Self-employed Women and Women in Informal Sector (1987) Shrama Shakti, New Delhi, pp. 350-351.
60. Boserup Ester(1970): *Women's Role in Economic Development,* London, George Allen and Unwin Limited, 1970.
61. Ramana and Krishna: *Urban Informal Sector: Some Issues.*
62. Blood and Wolfe (1958): *'The Effects of Wife's employment on the family power structure social forces"*, 36.
63. Gupta Sen, (1960): *Women Workers in India,* Asia Publishing House Bombay, p. 185.
64. Report of the Bureau – Working Class Women and Working Class Families in Bombay in *Economic and Political Weekly*, July 22 1978. p. 1169.
65. Thorner Alice (1985): Household as a First Stage in a Study of Urban Working Class Women, *Economic and Political Weekly.*
66. Nye F. and Hoffman (1963): *The Employed Mother in America,* Chicago.
67. Raj Gopalan C. (1963): *Social Change: An Analysis of Role conflict* and Rand McNally and Company. Deviation', *Indian Journal of Social Work*, pp. 12-13.
68. Kamal Nath.: Women in Working Force in India, *Economic and Political Weekly*, 1968. pp. 101. Women in Service Occupations, *Economic and Political Weekly*, 1967, pp. 25-27.

69. Chowdary, Sudheer (1969): *Women in Employment*, School of Social Work, Delhi,

70. Sen Gupta,Padmini: '*Women Workers in India*', Asia Publishing House, Bombay, 1960, p. 185.

71. Singh K.P: Career and Family, Women's Two Roles, *Indian Journal of Social Work*, 1972, 33(3), pp. 277 to 281.

72. Sinha and Ranade: *Women Construction Workers—Report of Two Surveys*, 1975.

73. Mazumdar: Women Workers in Changing Economy. *Yojana,* May 1975.

74. Kala Rani: *Role conflicts in Working Women*, Chetana Publications, NewDelhi,1976

75. Murali Manohar (1968): Women Construction Workers of Warangal, *International Labour Review*, Vol. 114, No.1 July-, August 1968, pp. 97-98.

76. Blumberg and Dwaraki (1980): *India's Educated Women: Options and Constraints*; Hindustan Publishing Corporation. Delhi.

77. Ranade and Ramachandran: *Women and Employment—Report of Pilot Bombay*, 1970. pp. 60.

78. Manohar: "Socio-Economic Status of Indian Women", *AIWC*, Delhi,1983, pp.78

79. Shervani, Modeeha: Why More Women Entering Work force? *Yojana,* June 1-15. 1984, pp. 23 to 28.

80. Gita Sen. and Chinranjeevi Sen.: Woman's Domestic Work Economic April 1985, *Economic and Political Weekly*, Vol., XX No. 17.

81. Thorner Alice and Joythi: Household as a first stage in a study of urban Working Class *Women in Economic and Political Weekly*, 1985.

82. Bandyo Padhyay, B: Women Worker in the Informal sector of Industry in Calcutta, *Journal of All India Woman's Association*, September 1929.

83. Kelsell et al: *The Sociology of an Elite*, London, Methuen & Co, Ltd.1972.

84. Uma Ramaswamy(1991): 'World and Development' , *The Indian Journal of labour Economics*, Vol.,34, No.3,1991

85. Saikia, Gogoi,Lekharu: "Indian Rural Woman", A study on Role and Status of Rural Women in Assam. Mittal Publications, New Delhi.

86. Vignaras Ponna: "Women Poverty and Resources", Sage Publications, New Delhi. New Beny Park, London, 1990.

87. Errol. D'Souza: World Employment ILO Perspectives: *Economic and Political Weekly,* September 26, 1998.

88. Thakur, K.: "Women and Development', *Case Study of Nauhatta Block*, Vikas Publishing House Pvt. Limited, New Delhi.

89. Papola,T.S.: Informal Sector, Concept and Policy, Special Articles, *Economic and Political Weekly*, Vol., XV. No.18.

90. Kamal Naryan Kabra, "Urban Poverty, Unorganised Sector and Self Employment Progammes for Urban and Urban Poor".(Ed) Centre for Urban Studies, *Indian Institute of Public Administration*, New Delhi, pp. 146-155.

91. Tara Kumari (1999), *Women in Urban India.*

92. K Viswanathan, Tharian George: Informal Labour Market and Structural.Development *Economic and Political Weekly*, August, 2003 Vol. XXXVIII No. 31.

93. Joythi Gupta: Informal Labouring Brick kilns need for Regulations, *Economic and Political Weekly*, Vol., XXXVIII, March 8, 2003.

94. A. Prakash and P.M. Mathew: "Urban Unemployment in Kerala", *Economic and Political Weekly*, March, 8, 2003.

95. Supriya Roy Chowdary: Old Classes and New Spaces Urban Poverty Unorganised Labour. *Economic and Political Weekly,* Vol., XXXVIII, No. 50.

96. Keshab Das (2003): *Informal Economy Centre Stage New structures of employment*. Sage Publications, New Delhi, 2003.

3

VISAKHAPATNAM: A PROFILE

The city of Visakhapatnam, the second largest city in the State of Andhra Pradesh next to Hyderabad, is located on the East Coast of India, mid-way between the metropolitan cities of Madras (Chennai) and Calcutta (Kolkotta). According to the Census of India (2001) it had a population of over a million and half enjoying the rank of 21st among all the cities in the country in 2001. Within the context of rapidly growing population, the Indian towns and cities are constantly growing, while some have been growing at a moderate rate, others are expanding rapidly, and one such rapidly expanding city is Visakhapatnam.

This chapter presents an analysis of Visakhapatnam city in terms of the people, economy, geographical features and the society.

Visakhapatnam-Vizag–Waltair

Visakhapatnam is an amalgamation of the old and the new where ancient temples lie in the shadows of gigantic Hindustan Shipyard. The city is a visitors' delight, with its beautiful beach, stretching endlessly against a backdrop of low hills, dotted with secluded caves and creeks. The 3rd century B.C. to 2nd century A.D. Buddhist ruins of Totlakonda and Bhavikonda are just at the outskirts of the city. Several Dutch and English buildings dated back to 17th and 18th century A.D are the highlights of the city.

The city's biggest advantage is its closeness to the most of the countries buzzling with activities in South Asia like Hong Kong, Singapore, Japan, Malaysia, Korea etc.

VISAKHAPATNAM: A Historic Profile

This city was ruled by several dynasties including famous Kalingas during 7th century AD, Chalukyas during 8th century AD, Rajahmundry reddy kings, Cholas, Golkonda Nawabs etc. The antiquity of the region is evident in its mention in the *Ramayana* and the *Mahabharata*. The former tells of the forests through which Lord Sri Rama travelled in search of His abducted wife Sita Devi, and where He met his devotee, Shabari, who directed Him to the mountains where Hanuman lived. Sri Rama also met Jambhavant, a bear man, who helped him in His battle with Ravana. It was heard too, that Bheema defeated the demon Bakasura. The Pandava's huge stone club can be seen in the village of Uppalam, 40 kms away. This region, formerly part of the great Kalinga Empire that stretched up to the Godavari, has also been mentioned in Hindu and Buddhist texts from the 5th and 6th centuries B.C, as well as by Sanskrit grammarians, like Panini, Katyayana etc. in the 4th century B.C. After Independence this was the biggest district in the country, which was then divided into different districts, viz. Srikakulam, Vijayanagaram and Visakhapatnam.

Size and situation

Visakhapatnam city is situated on the East Coast of India in between 17° 42' North latitude and 82° 2' East longitudes, at a distance of 860 km, from Kolkotta and 760 km, from Chennai. Visakhapatnam is one of the major ports in India. Besides this, the city has large public sector capital-intensive industries like Visakhapatnam Steel Plant (VSP), Hindustan Shipyard Limited (HSL), and Bharat Heavy Plate and Vessels Limited (BHPV) etc. Apart from this, Visakhapatnam is headquarters of the Eastern Naval Command of the Indian Navy, as also the Divisional headquarters of East Coast Railways and is also the seat of Andhra University. Further, the city is popularly known as Steel city or the city of Destiny. The total geographical area of the city is about 550 sq. km. According to 2001 census, the population of the city was around 15 lakhs and that of Visakhapatnam Urban Agglomeration (GVMC) is 20 lakhs now.

PHYSICAL CHARACTERISTICS OF THE CITY

Based on topographical conditions, the city and its environs can be divided into four categories, namely, hilly regions, uplands tracts, rolling plains and plains. The major hill ranges of the city are Kailasa range and Yarada range. The Kailasa range stretches from Simhachalam to Muvalavanipalem Colony, while on the other side, from Malkapuram to Gajuwaka on the south. A considerable number of hillocks and residual hills are found in various parts of the City. The rolling plains stretch from the foothills to the plains. The uplands tracts are found in the hillocks and residual hills. The altitude of Kailasa range is in between 0 to 507 meters above the mean sea level (MSL), while the altitude of Yarada ranges between 0 to 367 meters above MSL. The heights of residual hills and hillocks are less than 30 metres. The topography of the rolling plains has gentle to smooth undulation with an altitude of 20 to 30 metres above the MSL. The coastal plains are irregular with headlands, beach sand and mud flats.

Climate

Visakhapatnam and its environs come under semi-arid category. The mean annual range of temperature is as low as 18.4°C, which is a characteristic feature of coastal situation. May is the hottest month with the maximum temperature touching 34°C and January the coldest month with the minimum temperature of 14°C, the relative humidity is very high (80–84%) from April to September on account of monsoonal rains. The maximum rainfall (427mm) occurs in the months of September-October during the retreating monsoon period. October is the wettest month, with maximum rainfall of 259 mm, while January is the driest month with a minimum rainfall of only 7.2 mm. The climate of Visakhapatnam city is not extreme due to maritime conditions. Hence, the climate is comfortable and pleasant.

Soils

The main categories of soils in this city are red sands, alluvial and sediments, saline coastal sandy soils, skeletal soils etc. Red sandy soils, which cover 50 per cent of the tract, are associated with Khondalites and granite with high percentage of sand (80%) and low clay content (less than 15) with pH 7.0 to 8.0. The soil is usually associated with rolling plains, which are medium to fine in texture with pH 7.0 to 9.0. The coastal sandy soils are coarse to fine textured, rich in heavy minerals like monazite, yemenite and zircon with pH ranging from 6.5 to 8.0. Skeletal soils (colluviums and lateritic gravel) occur on eroded foot slopes of the hills. They are infertile, highly permeable with pH ranging from 4.0 to 6.0.

Drainage

Visakhapatnam and its environs have a fairly good surface drainage system. A number of non-perennial mountain streams and perennial spring waters contribute to the total drainage system of the area. All the streams follow gravity, the general slope directions of the tract before joining the Bay of Bengal. Mostly, the drainage pattern in the tract is dendrite and sub - pattern, which occur in the valleys of strike ridges and dissected pediments.

Vegetation

The vegetation in the tract is of tropical moist deciduous type. The soils support rich vegetation spots of thick foliage, both natural and orchard (mango, jack-fruit, cashew etc) are grown on the lower debris slope (5.15), where water trickles down in the form of springs. The dry deciduous and thorny forest is found at lower elevation hill slopes. Both dry and wet crops are cultivated in the plains. Most parts of the tract are strewn with small shrubs, and palymyrah trees. Maritime bushy grasses cover the coastal sand dunes. 'Avitinnia Alba' grows in the saline marshes. Coconut, cashew and casuarinas are grown on the beach and on the dune sands as commercial plantations.

Work Force

According to 2001 census, the work force in Visakhapatnam city was 2,18,695, (Table 3.1) and significant proportion are in trade and commerce (17.51%), transport

(16.75%) and industry (14.54%), while the lowest is found in cultivators group (0.15%) in 2001. The percentage share of work force is showing an increase during 1971-2001 in the workers' categories of livestock, (2.47 to 2.56), construction (7.53 to 7.60), trade and commerce (13.56 to 17.51) and other allied services (30.84 to 39.45). On the other hand, some other categories like house hold industry (1.30 to 0.56) and cultivators (0.52 to 0.15) other than household industry (16.00 to 14.54), are showed a decreasing trend in their shares during 1971-2001.

Table 3.1: Occupational Structure: 1971–2001

Sl. No	*Occupation*	*No of workers in 2001*	*% to the total workers*	*No. of workers in 1971*
1.	Cultivation	318	0.15	0.52
2	Agricultural	1,460	0.67	0.83
3	Livestock	5,605	2.56	2.47
4	Mining & Quarrying	458	0.21	0.43
5	Household Industry	1,232	0.56	1.30
6	Industrial workers	31,809	14.54	16.00
7	Construction	16,614	7.60	7.53
8	Trade & Commerce	38,309	17.51	13.56
9	Transport	36,611	16.75	26.52
10	Other	86,279	39.45	30.84
11	Total	2,18,695	100.00	100.00

Source: Hand book of Statistics-2001

Land-use Pattern

Comparative Land-use Statistics 1997 and 2002 (Area in Hectares)

The city has witnessed accelerated growth since mid 1990s. The proposals for further expansion of the steel plant, establishment of SEZ and the initiatives taken by the Central and State governments, as a result of economic reforms, to establish/expand medium to heavy industries in the spheres of chemicals (Petroleum),IT-based industries, Pharmaceuticals, etc might be the cause of this growth. Thus, land-use pattern data has been analysed. The comparative land use statistics at the point of time is presented in Table 3.2.

Table 3.2: Comparative Land-use statistics from 1997 and 2002

(Area in ha)

Sl. No	*Name*	*Area 2002 based on satellite imagery*	*Percentage to total*	*Area 1997*	*Percentage to total*
1.	Built up land	16601	9.58	15302	8.89
2.	Recreational/ open Space	2533	1.46	2759	1.60
3.	Transportation/ Communication	793	0.47	731	0.42
4.	Agricultural land	89712	51.98	90630	52.66
5	Forest land/hills	21100	12.26	18962	11.02
6.	Waste land	32203	18.77	34791	20..22
7.	Water Bodies	5397	3.13	5194	3.20
8.	River/streams	1804	1.05	1829	0.87
9.	Others	1957	1.13	1902	1.11
	Total	1,72,100	100.00	1,72,100	100.00

Source: Master Plan for VMR-2021.

Out of the total geographical areas of 1.72 ha lakhs the built up land has been increased from Ha 15302 ha in 1997 to 16601 ha in 2002 or from 8.89 per cent to 9.58 per cent of the geographical area, followed by recreational/open space was 2759 ha (1.60 %) which has been marginally decreased to 2533 ha constituting 1.46 per cent. Transportation and communication was with 731 ha (0.42%) in 1997 which has been slightly increased to 793 ha constituting 0.47 per cent in 2002. While, according to the satellite based imagery, agricultural land was 90630 ha (52.66%) in 1997 which has been decreased to 89712 ha (51.98%) during 2002.According to 1997 forestland/hills were 18962 ha constituting 11.02 per cent which has increased to 21100 ha with (12.26%). Waste land according to 1997 was

34971 ha (20.22%) which was decreased to 32203 ha constituting 18.77 per cent. Area of water bodies was Ha5194 (3.20%) which has been decreased to 5397ha (3.13%). Area of river/streams were 1829 ha (0.87%) in 1997 which has been increased to 1804 ha (1.05%). While, others in 1997 was Ha 1902 (1.11) per cent and increased to Ha 1957 (1.13) per cent in 2002.

Population

Table 3.3 presents the trends in population growth in the Visakhapatnam City. The population of the City in the beginning of the last century (1901) was only 40 thousand. The City population remained more or less stable up to 1921, but recorded a moderate growth during 1931-41, and an exploding growth after 1951, the highest decadal growth was reported, during 1951-1961 (95.47%). The Urban Agglomeration data are available from 1961 onwards. The period 1961-91, was experienced as the population explosion period, in which population has increased at a rate of growth of 7 per cent per annum, one of the highest in the Asian cities during the period. This is primarily because of the growth in the industrial activity. The growth rate was the lowest during 1991-2001 (25.76%).

Table 3.3: Population Growth in Visakhapatnam City

Year	*Population*	*Decadal variation*	*Percentage of growth*
1901	40,892	—	—
1911	43,413	+2,521	6.17
1921	44,711	+1,298	2.99
1931	57,303	+12,592	28.16
1941	70,243	+12,940	22.16
1951	1,08,042	+37,799	53.81
1961	2,11,190	+1,03,148	95.47
1971	3,55,045	+1,43,855	68.12
1981	6,75,163	+3,20,118	62.00
1991	10,57,118	+4,81,955	76.43
2001	13,29,472	+2,72,354	25.76

Source: Census of India, 1971, 1981, 1991 and 2001.

Population Growth in Major Metropolitan Cities in India

A comparison of proportionate population growth rate in major metropolis in India during 1991-2001 has revealed that Delhi has registered the highest growth rate with (52%), followed by Bombay (30%), Hyderabad (27%), Visakhapatnam (26%), Chennai (20.28%) and Kolkotta (17.19%). It is clear from the Table 3.4 that Visakhapatnam is among the top four cities in India in respect of high growth rate of population during 1991-2001.

Table 3.4:Population Growth in Major Metropolitan Cities in India

City	*2001*	*1991*	*Decennial growth rate (1991-2001)*
Delhi	1,27,91,458	8,375,188	51.93
Mumbai	1,63,68,084	12,567,978	29.94
Hyderabad	55,86,844	4,273,498	27.00
Visakhapatnam	13,29,472	10,57,118	25.76
Chennai	64,24,624	5,361,468	20.28
Kolkotta	1,32,16,546	10,860,399	17.19

Source: - Census of India 1991and 2001

Population Growth in Major Cities of Andhra Pradesh

While comparing the decadal growth rate of population for 1961-2001 of the major cities in Andhra Pradesh, it has been noticed that Tirupathi has registered the highest growth rate with 44 per cent, followed by Hyderabad (27 per cent), Visakhapatnam (26 per cent), Warangal (23 per cent), Rajahmundry (22%) and Vijayawada (20%). It is observed from the Table 3.5 that Visakhapatnam is among the top cities in Andhra Pradesh in respect of growth of population during 1961-2001.

Table 3.5: Population Growth in Major Cities of Andhra Pradesh Decadal Growth Rate

City	*1961-71*	*1971-81*	*1981-91*	*1991-2001*
Tirupathi	83.69	775.03	80.34	43.65
Hyderabad	43.83	40.74	61.54	27.00
Visakhapatnam	2.10	63.50	76.43	25.76
Warangal	32.94	61.92	69.36	23.40
Rajahmundry	45.23	41.81	51.27	21.56
Vijayawada	47.04	58.14	63.71	20.43

Source: - Census of India 1961, 1971, 1981, 1991 and 2001.

Growth Rate of Visakhapatnam City compared to other Cities in Andhra Pradesh

The growth of Visakhapatnam city while comparing with other cities of Andhra Pradesh, holds second rank with the population of 15,10,472 next to Hyderabad which is having a population of 55,86,844 and ranks first. Next to Visakhapatnam, Vijayawada holds the third rank with the population of 10,11,152 and Warangal holds fourth rank with the population of 5,77,190. While Guntur, having the population of 5,14,707 holds fifth rank among the different cities and Rajahmundry holds sixth rank with the population of 4,08,341 shown in Table 3.6.

Table 3.6: Growth of Visakhapatnam City comparison to other cities of Andhra Pradesh

City	*Population 2001*	*Rank*
Hyderabad	55,86,844	1
Visakhapatnam	15,10,472	2
Vijayawada	10,11,152	3
Warangal	5,77,190	4
Guntur	5,14,707	5
Rajahmundry	4,08,341	6

Source: - Census of India 2001.

Sex Ratio

Table 3.4 shows the sex ratio of Visakhapatnam City during the period 1951-2001. It can be easily found from the Table that the sex ratio of Visakhapatnam City has declined from 978 in 1951 to 920 in 1961 and then increased to 971 by 2001. It can also be observed from Table 3.7 that the ratio of females to males is very low in 1961 i.e., 920 females per 1000 males and very high in 1951 i.e. 978 females per 1000 males. Sex ratio of females to males is very low because of the proportion people living below poverty line is high and high infant mortality rate, extremely unhygienic conditions of living and absence of pre-natal and post- natal care. Besides this, high mortality rates among women in reproductive ages is also responsible for a declining female sex ratio.

Table 3.7: Sex Ratio in Visakhapatnam City

Year	*Sex Raiot (Females per,1,000 Males)*
1951	978
1961	920
1971	921
1981	925
1991	939
2001	971

Source: District Census Report of Andhra Pradesh, Govt. of India

Levels of Literacy

Table 3.8 presents the levels of literacy in Visakhapatnam city as a whole. The literacy rate is about 77.10 per cent in 2001 which shows an increasing trend compared to 1961 (48%). The female literacy rate is lower than that of males. The male literacy rate which was 31 per cent in 1961 shooted to 83.75 per cent by 2001. Similarly for females it was 17 per cent in 1961 and it tremendously increased to 70 per cent in 2001.

Table 3.8: Levels of Literacy in Visakhapatnam City: 1961-2001

	1961	*1971*	*1981*	*1991*	*2001*
Total male population	94,803	1,84,820	2,98,757	3,87,784	6,74,080
Total female population	87,201	1,70,225	2,76,406	3,64,253	6,55,392
Total population	1,82,004	3,55,045	6,75,163	10,57,118	13,29,472
Total maleliterates	55,542	1,14,073	1,97,893	3,12,370	5,64,676
Total female literates	31,090	68,244	1,30,513	2,31,119	4,60,347
Total literates	96,632	1,82,317	3,28,406	5,43,489	10,25,023
Non-literate males	39,261	70,747	1,00,864	75,414	1,09,404
Non-literate females	56,111	1,01,981	1,45,893	1,33,134	1,95,045
Total Non-leterates	95,372	1,72,827	2,46,757	2,08,548	3,04,449
% of literate males in Total population	30.52	32.13	34.41	41.51	83.75
% of literate females in Total population	17.09	19.23	22.70	30.71	70.24
% of total literate in Total population	47.61	51.36	57.11	72.22	77.10

Source: *Census of India* 1961, 1971, 1981, 1991 and 2001.

Education and Medical facilities

There are 3550 Primary Schools with 2.80 lakhs children on enrolment, 489 Upper Primary Schools with an enrolment of 1.28 lakhs, 447 High Schools with 2.04 lakhs pupils on roll, 196 Junior, Degree and Professional Institutions with 0.83 lakh students during 2002-2003. Regarding medical facilities, there are 159 Government Hospitals and dispensaries both Allopathic and Indian Medicine with 2819 bed strength and 596 doctors.

Power

Power consumption by industries in the city is 42.45 million kWh while it is 70.17 mkWh for Agricultural purposes in the District. All the 3,335 habitations in the District have been electrified including solar power system during 2002-2003.

Banking

There are 320 bank branches including Cooperative Banks in the District to look after the credit needs of the people.

Industries

Industrial development is conspicuous in Visakhapatnam urban agglomeration with the large scale industries like Hindustan Shipyard, Hindustan Petroleum Corporation Ltd, Coromandal Fertilizers Ltd, Bharath Heavy Plates and Vessels Ltd, L.G. Polymers Ltd; Hindustan Zinc Plant Ltd, , and recent giant Visakhapatnam Steel Plant and a host of other ancillary industries. The Visakhapatnam Steel Plant is the biggest with an authorised share capital of Rs.7466 crores with a licensed capacity of 2.8 millions tonnes of salable steel, 3.0 millions Tonnes of Pig Iron and 8.32 lakhs tonnes of by product. About 25,000 persons are expected to be employed. The Project has provided employment to 16300 persons. On the countryside the agro-based industries like sugar factories, jute mills and rice mills are established besides brick and tile units. The District has 1063 registered factories under the Factories Act functioning with a workforce of 77,203 persons during 2002-2003.

Communication

The district has a road length of 7336 km of which the National Highway No 5 runs to a length of 134.28 kms, State Highways at a length of 277 kms and the balance forms the roads maintained by Roads and Buildings, Zilla Praja Parishad and Mandal Praja Parishads. The number of vehicles registered during 2002-2003 were 390,322 of which 326,295 are Motor Cycles. There are 660 Post Offices, 7 Telegraph Offices and 96 Telephone Exchanges with 156,993 Telephone connections in the District.

City shifts from South to North

The City was once a small fishermen village, the old town area, until the British arrived here. They developed Bhimunipatnam as the port and Waltair uplands as their residential colony. The city extended up to Poorna Market, the only commercial center for the entire city even up to 1970. After construction of Jagadamba Theatre, the city moved towards north and the commercial activity spread up to the so-called Jagadamba center in 1970's. Thereafter the city expanded further northwards after the construction of the RTC Complex and the city's tallest building by the LIC in 1980's. The entire Dabagardens area had become a hub of electronic goods trade. In 1990's the prestigious NH-5 Project brought the city shift towards further to the north. With the proposed construction of I.T towers in the old TB Hospital area, the city is destined to create a hub for IT activity. The old town area is specialised in fishing.

Quality of life in Slums

This is briefly based on an evaluation study conducted by the Institute for Development and Planning Studies, Visakhapatnam. Table 3.9 presents the number of slums, households and population in Visakhapatnam Metropolitan Region. In the city itself there are 268 slums habitants 60,231 households with a population of 2,51,530. After the successful implementation of the slum improvement project in Hyderabad, the ODA (UK) sanctioned a similar project to Visakhapatnam

Table - 3.9: Trends in Socio-economic Indicators in Vizag Slums

Sl.	Socio-economic Indicators	1998		1991		1996	
		No.	%	No	%	No	%
1	**Demographic Change**						
	No. of sample households	612		612		300	
	Total sample population	2806		2889		1288	
	Average Household size	4.58		4.72		4.30	
2	**Education**						
	Literacy rate (overall)						
	Males	923	64.73	1093	74.00	494	75.54
	Females	585	42.39	725	51.34	380	59.94
	Total	1508	53.74	1818	62.93	874	67.86
	Literacy rate (15yrs & above						
	Males	524	61.00	632	67.38	366	87.14
	Females	245	28.13	316	34.96	240	58.82
	Total	769	44.45	948	51.47	606	73.19
	Literacy rate of S.C. Population (total)	289	50.44	388	63.82	441	50.46

(Contd...)

Table - 3.6: (Contd.)

SI.No	Socio- economic Indicators	1998		1991		1996	
		No.	%	No	%	No	%
3	**Housing and Environment**						
	Residence owning the house	533	87.09	542	88.56	267	89.00
	Households with Pucca houses	182	29.74	339	55.39	205	68.33
	S.C. household with pucca houses	26	19.85	78	59.54	97	69.78
	S.C household with separate latrine	72	11.76	133	21.73	70	23.33
	Households using tap water for drinking	325	53.10	345	56.37	166	55.33
	Household using dustbins	108	17.65	282	46.08	180	60.00
4	**Labour Force**						
	Gainfully employed (15yrs &above)						
	Males	715	83.24	743	79.21	373	88.81
	Females	182	20.89	224	24.78	175	42.79
	Total	897	51.85	967	52.49	548	66.10
5	**Incomes** (Rs)	1988	1991	1996			
	Per household real income	956		1108		1295	
	Per capita income	208		235		302	
	Per workers real income (earned_						

	Males	702		761		847	
	Females	313		312		415	
	Total	622		654		709	
	S.C. Per worker real income (earned)						
	Males	677		623		842	
	Females	251		324		377	
	Total	576		542		701	
6	**Income distribution** (Gini Co-efficient)	0.265		0.308		19.113	
	Health, status, immunizationand family planning						
	Fully immunized children(1-3yrs age)	56	24.67	92	82.88	32	96.97
	Partially immunized children(1-3yrs age)	152	66.96	18	16.22	1	3.03
	Not immunized children(1-3yrs)	19	8.37	1	0.90	0	0
	No. of vasectomies	106	35.22	106	27.18	50	28.09
	No. of Tubectomies	193	64.12	262	67.18	124	69.66
	Births attended by trained person at the house or residence	16	45.71	7	53.85	3	60.66
	General sickness(in last 14 days)	43	1.53	130	4.50	66	5.12

Source:- Institute for Development and Planning Studies, Visakhapatnam

in 1988-89. The major objective of the Visakhapatnam Slum Improvement Project (VSIP) was to meet the basic needs of the urban poor through physical improvement of slums and to improve the quality of life for nearly two lakhs people with an initial grant of Rs. 20.70 crores, out of which Rs. 15.67 crores (75.70%) was allotted to the improvement of physical infrastructure. The VSIP evaluation study observed that the physical infrastructure of slums has been totally changed. All the slums are provided with C.C. roads, streetlights, dustbins and protected water through pipelines. The quality of housing has improved with 55 per cent of households constructing pucca houses, and another 16 per cent have semi-pucca houses. The respondents reported that the house rents have recorded an increase from Rs.75 to Rs. 116 in 1991. With the increased access to the slums, frequent visits of the officials to the slums and skill improvement progammes, there was an increase in work participation rates and gainful employment. In 1991, nearly 50 per cent of the work force was engaged in unskilled labour and 25 per cent were in skilled jobs. However, women workers in skilled labour category were only about 4 per cent. Per household monthly income in real terms increased from Rs.956 in 1988 to Rs.1108 in 1991. Even though one cannot attribute this entirely to the VSIP. It is a remarkable improvement in the economic status of slum households. Development through community participation is the basic approach of the VSIP. It is reported that about three- fourths of the respondents are aware of the development programme, but only one – fifths have actually participated in them. Only about 60 per cent of the respondents reported the visit of Sanitary/Health officials of the Municipal Corporation. With the establishments of Primary Health Care Centers (PHCCs), people reported that death rate is decreasing day by day. Institutional deliveries have increased from 42 per cent in 1988 to 72 per cent in 1991. As much as 83 per cent of children were immunized fully. Family Planning acceptor rate has increased from 64 per cent in 1988 to 67 per cent in1991. The summative evaluation of the VSIP brings out clearly the substantial and significant improvement in physical and social infrastructure and in the levels of living of the slum dwellers particularly in the matters of housing, consumption expenditure, health, immunization of women and children, family planning and education. However the Study brings out certain features. The lowest income groups in the slum communities have not apparently shared adequately in the overall changes in the level of living. The relative disadvantage situation of the women folk in the slums in respect of occupation, wage earnings and vocational education has not improved. The Study also brought out that the community participation in the management of the newly created infrastructure has not shown any great improvement or strength. These findings should be matters of serious concern and the VMC should pay more attention in the future to rectify these inequalities and deficiencies.

4

SOCIO-ECONOMIC CHARACTERISTICS OF THE SAMPLE HOUSEHOLDS

Introduction

An attempt is made in this chapter to present the socio-economic status of the selected women in Visakhapatnam City. Variables such as age, education, social group, structure of the family, marital status, occupation etc., are considered as the important factors, contributing to the growth of urban informal activities. These social factors have greater impact on human beings, because they involve interaction with immediate human environment like family peers, caste, and religious groups and in the process of socialisation, family plays a vital role to a greater extent.

Social Background of the Selected Women by Religion

Woman workers in the urban informal sector are classified into six categories. The distribution of sample respondents based on their religion – Hindus, Christians, Muslims and others are presented in Table 4.1. This table indicated that among the total women workers, Hindus constitute 97 per cent, followed by Christians and Muslims. In the salaried workers' and domestic labourers' categories all are Hindus, closely followed by 98 per cent in the casual labourers' category, 97 per cent in the vendors' category, 94 per cent in the petty traders' category and 92 per cent of respondents are in the self employed category. All the Christians are in vendors' and petty traders' categories. All Muslims are in self-employed and petty traders categories.

From the Table, one can observe that Hindus are the dominant group in this area and therefore it has a bearing on the economic activities of women in the study area.

Table 4.1: Distribution of the Selected Women by Religion

Occupation	*Religion*				
	Hindu	*Christian*	*Muslim*	*Others*	*Total*
Petty traders	47 (94.00)	1 (2.00)	2 (4.00)	—	50 (100.00)
Vendors	121 (96.80)	4 (3.20)	—	—	125 (100.00)
Self-employed	23 (92.00)	—	2 (8.00)	—	25 (100.00)
Casual Labour	49 (98.00)	—	—	1 (2.00)	50 (100.00)
Domestic labour	25 (100.0)	—	—	—	25 (100.00)
Salaried workers	25 (100.0)	—	—	—	25 (100.00)
Total	290 (96.67)	5 (1.67)	4 (1.33)	1 (0.33)	300 (100.00)

Note: Figures in brackets indicate percentages to total numbers.

Distribution of the Selected Women by Caste

The selected woman respondent are divided into six categories as indicated earlier. Considering their caste as the major parameter, the details are presented in Table 4.2. It is observed that of the total respondents, 73 per cent belong to Backward Castes (B.C.s), followed by Schedule Castes (S.C.) (15%) and Other Castes (O.C.s.) (12%).

Among the six categories of workers, B.C.s are dominant in all the categories of worker with 84 per cent in domestic labourers', with 80 per cent in casual labourers', 75 per cent in vendors' categories 72 per cent in self-employed category, 64 per cent in petty traders' and 52 per cent in salaried workers' categories. S.C.s have followed B.C.'s with a major share in the salaried workers' category (28% share), 25 per cent among vendors', 16 per cent among domestic labourers', 12 per cent among casual labourers', 4 per cent each in petty traders', and in self -employed categories. The share of O.C's is lower with 32 per cent in petty traders', category, 24 per cent in self-employed category 20 per cent in salaried workers', 8 per cent in casual labourers' and with about 5 per cent in vendors' categories. It also indicated that these activities are centered on B.C's followed by S.C's. It is very clear from the Table that a majority of the selected women workers involved in unorganised sector are from the socially backward categories like B.C's and S.C's.

Table 4.2: Distribution of the Selected Women by Caste

Occupation	*Caste*			
	O.C	*B.C*	*S.C*	*Total*
Petty traders	16 (32.00)	32 (64.00)	2 (4.00)	50 (100.00)
Vendors	6 (4.80)	94 (75.20)	25 (20.00)	125 (100.00)
Self-employed	6 (24.00)	18 (72.00)	1 (4.00)	25 (100.00)
Casual Labour	4 (8.00)	40 (80.00)	6 (12.00)	50 (100.00)
Domestic Labour	—	21 (84.00)	4 (16.00)	25 (100.00)
Salaried Workers	5 (20.00)	13 (52.00)	7 (28.00)	25 (100.00)
Total	37 (12.00)	218 (73.00)	45 (15.00)	300 (100.00)

Note: Figures in parentheses indicate percentages to total numbers.

Marital Status of the Selected Woman Workers

Marital status of the respondents is presented in Table 4.3. It is observed from the table that out of the 300 respondents as many as 284 are married constituting 95 per cent of the total. Among these 284 respondents, 244 or about 81 per cent are united, while 40 respondents or 14 per cent of them are either widowed or divorced. Across the six working categories, all the respondents in the petty traders', casual labourers and domestic labourers categories are married. In the petty traders' category, two per cent of them are widows.

Whereas in the vendors' category, 95 per cent of them are married, 72 per cent are united, 3 per cent of are divorced and 20 per cent are widows. 'Regarding the self-employed category,

Table 4.3: Distribution of the Selected Women by Marital Status

	Marital status					
	Married					
Occupation	*United*	*Divorced*	*Widowed*	*Total*	*Un-married*	*Grand total*
Petty traders	49 (98.00)	—	1 (2.00)	50	—	50 (100.00)
Vendors	90 (72.00)	4 (3.20)	25 (20.00)	119	6 (4.80)	125 (100.00)
Self-employed	20 (80.00)	2 (8.00)	2 (8.00)	24	1 (4.00)	25 (100.00)
Casual Labour	46 (92.00)	—	4 (8.00)	50	—	50 (100.00)
Domestic Labour	24 (96.00)	—	1 (4.00)	25	—	25 (100.00)
Salaried Workers	15 (60.00)	—	1 (4.00)	16	9 (36.00)	25 (100.00)
Total	244 (81.34)	6 (2.00)	34 (11.33)	284 (94.67)	16 (5.33)	300 (100.00)

Note: Figures in parentheses indicate percentages to total numbers.

80 per cent of them are united and eight per cent of them are widowed, and four per cent of them are unmarried. Among casual labourers' category, 92 per cent of them are united and 8 per cent of them are widowed. In case of the domestic labourers' category, 96 per cent of them are married, four per cent of them are widows. Regarding the salaried workers' category, 60 per cent of the respondents are married and four per cent of them are widows, and 36 per cent of the respondents are unmarried.

It shows that marriage seems to be the main factor, which compelled the women folk to enter the workforce. The income earned by women could supplement the family income in terms of food, children's education, social obligations, and some times even to acquire assets also. Widows and divorcees work for their bare necessities of life, as they have to reconstruct their family without depending either on their parents or on any others to rear up their children and for their livelihood. Mostly, unmarried women respondents enter the workforce to supplement parents' income and for their own basic needs and they are predominantly seen in the category of salaried workers, because of their communication skills and lesser family responsibilities.

Age-wise Distribution of the Selected Woman

Age-wise distribution of the selected women is another important aspect, because age determines the motive for work participation. Hence, age-wise classification of the women working in urban informal sector is presented in Table 4.4. Out of the total 300 respondents, 50 per cent are in the age- group of 26-35, followed by 21 per cent of the women in the age group of 16-25, 20 per cent are in the age-group of 36-45 and 6 per cent of the respondents are in the age-group of 46-55. A more or less similar picture is emerged in other categories also. In the salaried workers' category, those in the 16-25 age-group predominate. There is only one woman in the age-group of 66 and above in the vendors' category.

Length of Service of the Selected Woman Workers

A worker may stick to the same work, profession, or economic activity mainly because of some reasons. They are as follows: Firstly, due to job satisfaction or earning more income than in the previous occupation. Secondly, lack of required technical skill, or there might be no alternative job. Thirdly, lack of required education might cause her to continue in the same work to earn income for the family. (Table 4.5) this can be explained with the help of length of service of women workers as presented in the table. It is found that, 38 per cent of women workers have below five years length of service, followed by 30 per cent with 6-10 years of service, 14 per cent with 11-15 years of service, 9 per cent with 16-20 years, 7 per cent with the service of 21-25 years and it is gratifying to note that 2 per cent of them have a service of 26 years and above. Among those with below 5 years of service, 72 per cent each belong to either self- employed category, or to the domestic labourers' category and 64 per cent each are from the petty traders' and salaried workers' categories. Except in the casual labourers' category of

Table 4.4: Age-wise Distribution of the Selected Women

Occupation	Age group (years)							
	Below-15	*16-25*	*26-35*	*36-45*	*46-55*	*56-65*	*66-above*	*Total*
Petty traders	—	18 (36.00)	30 (60.00)	2 (4.00)	—	—	—	50 (100.00)
Vendors	—	13 (10.40)	56 (44.80)	34 (27.20)	13 (10.40)	8 (6.40)	1 (0.80)	125 (100.00)
Self Employed	—	6 (24.00)	17 (68.00)	1 (4.00)	1 (4.00)	—	—	25 (100.C0)
CasualLabour	—	8 (16.00)	27 (54.00)	14 (28.0)	1 (2.00)	—	—	50 (100.00)
Domestic Labour	—	6 (24.00)	15 (60.00)	2 (8.00)	2 (8.00)	—	—	25 (100.00)
SalariedWorkers	—	12 (48.00)	5 (20.00)	8 (32.00)	—	—	—	25 (100.00)
Total	—	63 (21.00)	150 (50.00)	61 (20.33)	17 (5.67)	8 (2.67)	1 (0.33)	300 (100.00)

Note: Figures in parentheses indicate percentages to total numbers.

workers, the rest of them are equally distributed among different categories of workers in the 6-10 years of service. Among the ranges of 11-15 and 16-20 years of service, the vendors' category has reported the highest percentage. This is because women workers continue in the job as long as they are physically fit and have the capacity to work, which is quite true for youngsters. As they grow old, they may not be able to withstand the hard physical labour involved.

Table 4.5: Length of Service of the Selected Woman

Occupation	Length of Service (years)						
	Below-5	*6-10*	*11-15*	*16-20*	*21-25*	*26-above*	*Total*
Petty traders	32 (64.00)	14 (28.00)	3 (6.00)	1 (2.00)	—	—	50 (100.00)
Vendors	5 (4.00)	30 (24.00)	38 (30.40)	25 (20.00)	21 (16.80)	6 (4.80)	125 (100.00)
Self-employed	18 (72.00)	5 (20.00)	2 (8.00)	—	—	—	25 (100.00)
Casual labour	24 (48.00)	26 (52.00)	—	—	—	—	50 (100.00)
Domestic labour	18 (72.00)	7 (28.00)	—	—	—	—	25 (100.00)
Salaried Workers	16 (64.00)	9 (36.00)	—	—	—	—	25 (100.00)
Total	113 (37.67)	91 (30.30)	43 (14.33)	26 (8.67)	21 (7.00)	6 (2.00)	300 (100.00)

Note: Figures in parentheses indicate percentages to total numbers.

Working Hours in Respective Economic Activity of the Selected Woman Workers

The question of hours of work in a particular employment is also an important aspect for consideration. Adequate legislative provisions in ameliorating their socio-economic conditions have not covered the unorganised sector or what we call informal sector very effectively. Organised sector is the sector where statutory laws determine the working hours i.e., maximum of 48 hours per week with a weekly holiday. However, there are no such provisions in the unorganised sector, where the employers and intermediaries determine working hours. Table 4.6 provides information on the working hours of the women respondents in urban informal sector of Visakhapatnam.

Table 4.6: Working Hours in Respective Economic Activity of the Selected Woman Workers

	Working Hours (per day)					
Occupation	*Below-8*	*8-hours*	*9-10*	*11-12*	*12-above*	*Total*
Petty traders	49 (98.00)	—	1 (2.00)	—	—	50 (100.00)
Vendors	1 (0.80)	46 (36.80)	59 (47.20)	18 (14.40)	1 (0.80)	125 (100.00)
Self-employed	1 (4.00)	6 (24.00)	16 (64.00)	2 (8.00)	—	25 (100.00)
Casual labour	—	48 (96.00)	2 (4.00)	—	—	50 (100.00)
Domestic labour	25 (100.0)	—	—	—	—	25 (100.00)
Salaried workers	—	25 (100.0)	—	—	—	25 (100.00)
Total	76 (25.33)	125 (41.67)	78 (26.00)	20 (6.67)	1 (0.33)	300 (100.00)

Note: Figures in parentheses indicate percentages to total numbers.

It can be found from the Table that out of 300 respondents, 42 per cent of the respondents are working 8 hours per day and another quarter of them are working either 9-10 hours or less than 8 hours per day. As expected, vendors work for more than 11 hours per day compared to others. Similarly, in the case of self-employed category.

7. Educational Levels of the Selected Woman

Literacy is an important factor for creating a base for development. On one hand, it improves people's skills and on the other enables them to participate in modern economic activities successfully. Economists have long since recognised the importance of education in the development process.

Adam Smith considered that investment in education for acquiring ability as fixed capital. Alfred Marshall asserted that the most valuable of all capital is investment in human beings. T.W Schultz has shown the relation of economic development of industrialised economics and education. Harbinson and Myres consider that without investment in education, rapid economic development is not possible. Arthur Lewis asserted that poverty in some countries persists due to ignorance. Education is considered as a prime requirement in the development of human resources. The Government of India has established a new Ministry for the development of Human Resources (HR) by giving importance to the primary level education in the total programme. Similarly, the International Bank for Reconstruction and Development (IBRD) has started attached importance to the development of HR, particularly through education progammes since 1980's. Education develops the potential of a woman and also helps her understand herself and that of her environment, and fix goals for her life. Moreover, a child is likely to learn much from the mother than from others. Hence, education helps a woman in using her potential, and to become more receptive or open to new ideas whereby she will be willing to change and develop her analytical and conceptual skills, which helps her in understanding environment in a scientific manner. Education also develops alternatives to solve problems, improves communication skills, to be more responsive to the social obligations, learn to deal with others, and make use of the opportunities. Education of women can have a significant impact on the family atmosphere also. Education of the family and efficiency of the women workers can be recognised through education levels of women which have improved significantly in recent years. Still a majority of the working women in informal sector are illiterates.

The women in urban informal sector of Visakhapatnam City are not an exception to this trend. Table 4.7 explains the educational status of the respondents. It is found that out of the 300 respondents, 204 respondents are illiterates constituting 68 per cent, while 17 per cent of them have secondary level of education. Across the selected categories, in petty traders' category 44 per cent of them had primary level of education followed by a quarter of them with secondary level of education, and as much as 16 per cent are illiterate. Only in the petty traders' and self- employed workers' categories, one can find respondents with education up to higher secondary level. All those who are in the domestic labourers' and almost all in the casual labourers' categories are illiterates. At the other extreme, all the salaried workers reported that they had secondary school background and above.

Table 4.7: Distribution of the Selected Woman by Education

	Educational Status					
Occupation	*Illiterate*	*Literate*	*Primary*	*Secon-dary*	*H. Secondary*	*Total*
Petty traders	8 (16.00)	4 (8.00)	22 (44.00)	12 (24.00)	4 (8.00)	50 (100.00)
Vendors	122 (97.60)	—	3 (2.40)	—	—	125 (100.00)
Self-employment	2 (8.00)	—	7 (28.00)	14 (56.00)	2 (8.00)	25 (100.00)
Casual labour	47 (94.00)	3 (6.00)	—	—	—	50 (100.00)
Domestic labour	25 (100.00)	—	—	—	—	25 (100.00)
Salaried workers	—	—	—	25 (100.00)	—	25 (100.00)
Total	204 (68.00)	7 (2.33)	32 (10.67)	51 (17.00)	6 (2.00)	300 (100.00)

Note: Figures in patentheses indicate percentages to total numbers.

Distribution of the Selected Women by Language

India is a country with many of the languages. Each state has its own language or two. Among these languages, English and Hindi are the most common languages to all the citizens. Language is the communication link, and without which inter-personal interaction is not possible. Knowledge of no of languages entitles a person for better communication, which helps in tackling various situations at various places. Knowledge of different languages helps people to know of different cultures, traditions, and feelings. Knowledge of different languages reduces the communication gap between each other. Knowledge of different languages helps people in business deals. Table 4.8 explains the process of communication skills by way of different languages known to them. Out of 300 respondents, 183 members i.e., 61 per cent are illiterate and can speak Telugu only, and only a fifth of them can speak in both Telugu and Hindi, while 11 per cent of them can communicate in both Telugu and English indicating that communication skills are mostly confined to only one language. In the case of petty traders', vendors', casual labourers', domestic labourers' categories Telugu is the only one language known to all. However, regarding other categories, either of Telugu or Hindi, or English is the major languages known to them. In the petty traders' category, 24 per cent can speak only Telugu.

Table 4.8: Distribution of Selected Woman by Language Known

Occupation	*Languages Known*				
	Telugu	*Telugu & Hindi*	*Telugu & English*	*Telugu & Other Languages*	*Total*
Petty traders	27 (54.00)	12 (24.00)	6 (12.00)	5 (10.00)	50 (100.00)
Vendors	97 (77.60)	19 (15.20)	—	9 (7.20)	125 (100.00)
SelfEmployed	—	12 (48.00)	9 (36.00)	4 (16.00)	25 (100.00)
Casual Labour	40 (80.00)	10 (20.00)	—	—	50 (100.00)
Domestic Labour	19 (76.00)	6 (24.00)	—	—	25 (100.00)
Salaried Workers	—	5 (20.00)	17 (68.00)	3 (12.00)	25 (100.00)
Total	183 (61.00)	64 (21.33)	32 (10.67)	21 (7.00)	300 (100.00)

Note: Figures in parentheses indicate percentages to total numbers.

In case of vendors' category 78 per cent can speak only in Telugu, while 15 per cent can speak in Telugu and Hindi. In the self-employed workers' category, 48 per cent of them can speak in both Telugu and Hindi, and another 36 per cent have an idea of communicating in both Telugu and English. Among the casual labourers' category, 80 per cent can speak in Telugu and 20 per cent of them can speak in both Telugu and Hindi. In case of domestic labourers' category, 76 per cent of them are able to communicate only in Telugu and 24 per cent of them can communicate both in Telugu and Hindi. In the salaried workers' category, 68 per cent of them are able to communicate both in Telugu and English, while another 20 per cent of them can speak in Telugu and Hindi.

Distribution of the Selected Woman Workers by Skills

Formal education, skills, and previous work experience is considered important assets for the success of any workers. Training helps her in knowing the ins and outs of the work and adds a practical dimension to knowledge. Skilled persons try to improve their performance to increase income. Skill and technical knowledge are important factors that influence the quality of any worker. Majority of the women do not have any skills and technical knowledge. Still they work for economic reasons. They are unable to develop themselves without proper skills, because firstly they are illiterate; secondly, they are poor. The main aim is to supplement family earnings. In spite of the fact that they do not have skills, they are contributing to the family income and for the upgradation of their family status. This can be observed from Table 4.9. Out of 300 respondents, 66 per cent of them are working without any skill, whereas 19 per cent of them are engaged in their caste- based work, while nine per cent of them are semi-skilled and only 6 per cent have undergone any special training. Only in case of self-employed, casual labourers' and salaried workers' categories the respondents have reported any skills.

Table 4.9: Distribution of the Selected Woman by Skills

Occupation	*Skills*				
	Skilled	*Semi-skilled*	*Un skilled*	*Caste based*	*Total*
Petty traders	—	—	42 (84.00)	8 (16.00)	50 (100.00)
Vendors	—	—	75 (60.00)	50 (40.00)	125 (100.00)
SelfEmployed	16 (64.00)	9 (36.00)	—	—	25 (100.00)
CasualLabour	1 (2.00)	10 (20.00)	39 (78.00)	—	50 (100.00)
Domestic Labour	—	—	25 (100.00)	—	25 (100.00)
Salaried Workers	—	7 (28.00)	18 (72.0)	—	25 (100.00)
Total	17 (5.67)	26 (8.67)	199 (66.33)	58 (19.33)	300 (100.00)

Note: Figures in parentheses indicate percentages to total numbers.

Distribution of the Selected Women by Family Education Status

Family plays a vital role in the society and it is the important unit in the society. A woman can be influenced to work with dedication only when the family supports her like a backbone. Women can perform the work efficiently only with the encouragement from all the other family members. Despite the household chores women in urban informal sector work hard to earn for their families. Many empirical studies show that even though women earn less than men for the family, they save some part of the income and invest that amount in household activities whereas males spend their income on unproductive / unsocial activities like gambling, drinking or for personal entertainment. Table 4.10 presents some information on educational status of the family members of the respondents. From the sample population of 1214, members, 64 per cent are literates and 36 per cent of them are illiterates. It is found to be better compared to the women workers themselves. While the women workers had reported that only 32 per cent of them were literates their family members reported as much as 64 per cent as literates. Educated family members try to change their living conditions by changing their environment, style, pattern and about the alarming explosion of population.

Table 4.10: Distribution of the Selected Woman by Family Education Status

Occupation	*No of Households*	*Total members in the family*	*Family size*	*Illiterates*	*Literates*
Petty traders	50 (100.00)	200	4.00	29 (14.50)	171 (85.50)
Vendors	125 (100.00)	521	4.17	242 (46.45)	279 (53.55)
Self-employed	25 (100.00)	90	3.60	8 (9.00)	82 (91.00)
Casual Labour	50 (100.00)	206	4.12	91 (44.17)	115 (55.83)
Domestic labour	'25 (100.00)	85	3.40	50 (58.83)	35 (41.17)
Salaried workers	25 (100.00)	112	4.48	22 (19.64)	90 (80.36)
Total	300 (100.00)	1214	4.05	442 (36.40)	772 (63.60)

Note: Figures in parentheses indicate percentages to total numbers.

The average family size for the entire population is found to be 4.05 and it is more or less uniform for all the categories. Only in the case of domestic labourers' and self-employed categories it is slightly lower. In the case of salaried workers' category, it is found to be the highest (4.48). One point clearly emerges from the analysis. The women workers, though a majority of them are illiterates, are giving importance to educate their children as indicated by higher proportion of literates in the family.

Table 4.11: Work Participation Rates and Dependents Ratios among the Selected Women

Occupation	*Dependents*			*Earners*			*Average per Family*			
	Male	*Female*	*Total*	*Male*	*Female*	*Total*	*Dependents Ratio*	*Dependent*	*Earners*	*Family size*
Petty Traders	53(26.50)	47(23.50)	100(50.00)	50(25.00)	50(25.00)	100(50.00)	1.00	2.00	2.00	4.00
Vendors	132(25.34)	129(24.76)	261(50.09)	124(23.80)	136(26.11)	260(49.91)	1.00	2.09	2.08	4.17
Self Employed	19(21.11)	24(26.67)	43(47.78)	20(22.23)	27(30.00)	47(52.22)	0.91	1.72	1.88	3.60
Casual Labour	63(30.58)	43(20.87)	106(51.46)	49(23.78)	51(24.76)	100(48.54)	1.06	2.12	2.00	4.12
Domestic Labour	21(24.70)	13(15.29)	34(40.00)	25(29.41)	26(30.59)	51(60.00)	0.66	1.36	2.04	3.40
Salaried Workers	30(26.78)	28(25.00)	58(51.78)	24(21.43)	30(26.78)	54(48.22)	1.07	2.32	2.16	4.48
Total	318(26.19)	284(23.39)	602(49.59)	292(24.05)	320(26.36)	612(50.41)	0.98	2.00	2.04	4.05

Note: Figures in parentheses indicate percentages to total numbers

Work Participation Rates and Dependents Ratio among the Selected Women

Generally grand parents, parents, the couple, children and grand children constitute a family. Mainly the grandparents who are above 60 years of age and children aged below 15 years are considered dependents in the family and all others between 15 and 60 years are considered earners in the family. However, in this Study children who are above 15 years and who are studying are considered as dependents. As such, the entire family members are categorised as either dependents or workers. Mostly in India, one finds that dependents ratios are higher than earners ratio because of the fact that joint family system is still prevailing in our Country. Table 4.11, shows the work participation rates and dependent ratio among workers at family level. It is quite interesting to note that the dependent ratio is higher in case of salaried workers' category (1.07 per cent) followed by casual labourers' (1.06 per cent). The ratio is more or less same in petty traders' and vendors' categories (1.00 per cent), in the self- employed category the ratio is about (0.91 per cent), and it is the lowest in domestic labourers' category (0.66 per cent). Average per family earners are also higher in the salaried workers' category (2.16), followed by vendors', domestic labourers' and it is the lowest in the self-employed category. Average per family dependants are also higher in the salaried workers' category (2.32) followed by casual labourers', petty traders', vendors', self-employed and domestic labourers'categories. A more or less similar picture emerges from an analysis, which is based on categorisation of workers and dependents.

Summary

The growth and development is based absolutely on the social factors. The study revealed that among the total workers, Hindus constitute 97 per cent, followed by Christians and Muslims. In salaried workers' and domestic labourers' categories all are Hindus, closely followed by 98 per cent in the casual labourers' category, and it is more than 90 per cent in the vendors', petty traders', self-employed, categories. In almost all the categories a majority of the respondents are from backward castes and they dominant in all categories of workers. S.C's have followed B.C.'s with a major share in salaried workers' category with 28 per cent, The share of O.Cs' is lower with 32 per cent in petty traders' category, 24 per cent in self- employed category 20 per cent in salaried workers', 8 per cent in casual labourers', with about five per cent in vendors' categories.

Across the six selected categories as many as 284 (constituting 95 per cent of the total) are married and among them 244 (constituting 81%) are united, while 40 (constituting 14%) are either divorced or widowed. Education develops the potential and helps a person to be creative. Education and growth are inter-related with each other and it is also observed that out of 300 respondents, 204 are illiterates (68%), 17 per cent of them had secondary level of education, followed by 11 per cent with primary level of education. Almost all the workers from salaried workers' category had secondary level education. Regarding communication skills 54 per cent of the respondents from petty traders' category can speak only in Telugu, 78 per cent from vendors' category are able to speak only in Telugu, while, rest of them can speak both in Telugu and Hindi. Further 24 per cent of them from petty traders' category are able to speak only Telugu. Regarding acquisition of skills, only 9 per cent of them are semi skilled and another 6 per cent have under gone any special training. It is quite interesting to note that dependency ratio is higher in salaried workers' category (1.07%), followed by casual labourers (1.06%) and it is more or less similar in vendors' and petty traders' categories,(1.00% each), and quite low in domestic labourers' category (0.66%).

5
MIGRATION

Introduction

Migration means a change in, or shift, other than casual residence, from one location or settlement to another, involving movement across an administration border. The administrative border may be that of a village, a district, a state or a nation. Since times immemorial, man is restlessly migrating from one place to another as part of a process of adaptation to his social, economic, cultural and ecological environment. In the most primitive society, migration is the first mode of existence of the man. People used to migrate from one place to another in search of food, livelihood and security. Now, man is aiming to have a stable and stationary life which is more secured and developed, when compared to the life in the primitive society.

The word "migration" has been derived from the Latin Word '*migrare*' which means to change one's residence. Literally, it means settlement or shifting of an individual or a group of individuals from one cultural area or place of habitation to another. Migration is considered in the present study from the view point of its impact on income and living. An attempt has been made in this chapter to analyse the impact of migration on women who have settled in urban areas in general and in Visakhapatnam city in particular.

Concept of Migration

The concept of migration covers a change of milieu, i.e., environment, migration of people for food, shelter, security or other reasons. It has been an universal phenomenon. Donald[1] defined migration as a result of a conscious decision taken after a consideration or calculation of the advantages and disadvantages of moving and staying. According to Thomas[2] migration means change in, or shift other than casual, of residence from one location or settlement to another involving movement across an administrative border. The administrative border may be that of a village, district or state or nation, as noted earlier. In the view of Theodore[3] "Migration is, strictly speaking, a change of residence and need not necessarily involve any change of occupation, but it is closely associated with the occupational shifts of one kind or another".

According to Everett Lee[4] migration may be defined broadly "as a permanent or semi-permanent change of residence". Peterson[5] defined migration as "movement motivated by the individuals' willingness to risk, the unknown, of a new home and breaking from a familiar social universe for the sake of adventure, achievements of ideals or to escape a social system from which he has become alienated". In the words of Helen[6], "Migration is normally viewed as an economic phenomenon". Though non-economic factors obviously have some bearing, most studies concur that migrants leave their area of origin primarily for lack of employment opportunities.

Beijer[7], observed, "Migration is a necessary element of normal population redistribution and an arrangement for making use of the available manpower".

Jansen[8] regarded migration "as a demographic problem which influences the size of population at both the places, the place of origin as well as destination". According to Keneth Kamneyer[9], Migration is a relatively permanent moving away of collectively called migrants from one geographical location to another, preceded by decision making on the part of the migrants on the basis of hierarchically ordered set of values or value ends and resulting in changes in the international system of the migration". In general usage, the term has been restricted to relatively permanent change.

The term "Migration" has been defined in the Websters[10] Dictionary[10] as "the act or an instance of moving from one country, region or place to settle in another in search of work".

According to the *Multilingual Demographic Dictionary of the United Nations*[11] "Migration is a force of geographical mobility or spatial mobility between one geographical unit and another, generally involving a change in residence from the place of origin or place of departure to the place of destination or place of arrival. Such migration is called permanent migration and should be distinguished from other forms of movement which do not involve a permanent change of residence.

Chauhan[12] regards migration as a change of residence from one geographical area to another for a more than certain specified period of time".

Upreti[13] viewed "Migration as both a consequence and cause of social change" Thus, migration is viewed as a shift from one place to another to avoid the social and demographic problems and seek better economic opportunities, ultimately leading to social change.

According to Unnithan[14] Migration is a search for economic emancipation and migration is a dynamic social phenomenon which assumes great significance in the context of social, cultural and economic development.

Types of Migration

Migration can be classified into different types on the basis of physical distance, duration and the period of stay, cultural and political differences between the two places and individual, family and group and on the place where from the migrants come and where they settle.

According to Smith[15] there are three types of migration:

Migration from country to city (rural to urban)

Migration from city to country (urban to rural)

Migration from one province to another province,

Migration is also classified as

Free migration. and

Forced migration.

Free migration takes place as a result of the operation of

the free will and personal choice of the people and forced migration takes place as a result of political disturbances, dreadful droughts and famines.

Kingsley[16] observes five types of migration:-

Conquest.

Displacement

Forced labour

Free individual and

Controlled

Zachariah[17], has classified migration on the basis of the distance of movement such as short distance migration and long distance migration

Peterson[18] observed five types of migration namely:-

Primitive migration

Forced migration

Impelled migration

Free migration and

Mass migration

Census of India[19] classified internal migration into four types namely

Rural to urban

Rural to rural

Urban to urban and

Urban to rural

According to Tara Kumari[20] migrations are of three types viz,

Permanent

Seasonal and

Half seasonal

Thus, migration could be classified based on distance, period of stay, region, cultural differentials and purpose of movement. Among all types of migration, rural to urban is the most common phenomenon of the modern world, specifically in the developing world. In the Indian context, rural to urban migration is the most common feature.

Causes of Migration

Economic and non-economic factors are identified as the main causes of migration. The causes of rural-urban migration in India vary from region to region, due to the regional differences in economic activities, natural resources, social and cultural differences and the impact of various developmental activities. According to Kingsley[21] religious festivals, commercial fairs, dire famines, general wars and ruthless taxation in the past have accelerated the movement of population. During the British Rule, certain other conditions that favoured migration are development of the means of transport and communication, educational facilities, the decline of caste and family solidarity, the growth of large scale industries, the development of cities, the expansion of irrigation and increase in security. Majumdar[22] listed the following as causes of migration: Insufficiency of cultivable land, disputes in the family, presence of friends and relatives which might help the migrants to get a job, ruination of the hereditary occupation and loss of business, the attraction of city life, the absence of employment opportunities commensurate with their education in their native places, the desire for investment, official transfer, search for employment, political reasons and accompanying other elderly migrants. Dhekney[23] pointed out several causes of migration, of which the most important were as follows: securing employment, better prospects, better employment or better business, city- ward migration motivated by factors such as famine, inadequacy of land, loss of land and low income. Theadore Caplow[24] stated that "Migration", is strictly speaking a change of residence and need not necessarily involve only change of occupation, but it is closely associated with occupational shifts of one kind or another".[25]

It is also widely quoted in literature that family disputes, allurement of city life, commercial fairs, wars and famines, family size and its structure, social factors outside their villages such as educational prospects for children, entertainment opportunities strongly contribute to migration. Presence of friends and relatives in towns who help in getting jobs and political factors may also hasten up migration.

They may be summarised as follows:

- Social factors including the desire of migrants to break away from traditional constraints of social organisations.
- Physical factors including disasters like floods and droughts.
- Demographic factors including the concomitant high rates of rural population growth.
- Cultural factors including the security of "extended family" relationships and the allurement of "bright city life" and
- Communication factors including improved transportation, urban-oriented educational systems, and the 'modernising' impact of the introduction of radio, TV and the cinema.

Thus, migration implies mobility of generally able- bodied people in the working age-group in search of higher income opportunities and migration is a complex socio-economic phenomenon determined by several factors – natural, economic, social and inspirational. Mainly economic causes make people to migrate from one place to another.

Migration of Women

Migration of poor families from countryside to urban sites in search of livelihood and employment is a regular phenomenon in the economic life of India. The backwardness in agriculture, lack of irrigation facilities and famines have made a hazardous effect on the income and lives of poor peasants, and landless agricultural labourers. The result is unending migration to the towns in search of better life. Women are also part of those poor families who experienced the sorts of hardships along with men and in few cases women exclusively are found migrating to other areas leaving their parents, husbands and children at native villages. There has been a significant empirical evidence on women's work and their migration. In the traditional rural sector, women significantly work as 'free wage labourers' or permanently bondage labour though the income derived thereby is insignificant. Further, seasonal fluctuations in employment are high for women. Various socio-economic, cultural and psychological factors hinder the development of women. In such a situation, women migrate in search of better income-earning opportunities and thereby better levels of living.

With this brief review of literature on migration an attempt is made in this chapter to analyse the reasons for migration or other wise of the selected women respondents in the Visakhapatnam city. Information on occupational details, status of the migration before migration, type of migration etc was also elicited from the respondents.

Occupational Details of the Migrants and Non-Migrants

Prior to the causes for migration, an analysis of the proportion of the migrant households in the sample study is carried out to elicit the extent of migration in the study area. This may help in identifying the economic activities attracting migrants or observing migrants. The magnitude of migrants in the total sample are presented in Table 5.1.

Table 5.1: Composition of the Migrants and Non-Migrants

Occupation	*Migrants*	*Non -migrants*	*Total*
Petty Traders	18 (36.00)	32 (64.00)	50 (100.00)
Vendors	17 (13.60)	108 (86.40)	125 (100.00)
Self-Employed	18 (72.00)	7 (28.00)	25 (100.00)
Casual labour	47 (94.00)	3 (6.00)	50 (100.00)
Domestic labour	25 (100.00)	—	25 (100.00)
Salaried workers	8 (32.00)	17 (68.00)	25 (100.00)
Total	133 (44.34)	167 (55.66)	300 (100.00)

Note: Figures in parentheses indicate percentages to total numbers.

It can be observed from the Table, that 133 respondents are migrants, (constituting 44%). Among different occupations, the highest proportions of migrants are recorded in domestic labourers' category (100%), followed by casual labourers' (94%), self-employed (72%) categories and the lowest in the vendors' category (14%). As elicited from the respondents, lack of work at their native place and also low wages in the rural areas have forced both casual labourers and domestic labourers to migrate from rural areas to the city seeking better wages. Women working as casual labourers and domestic labourers are mostly illiterate and unskilled and tend to migrate from rural areas to urban areas for want of work and livelihood which they could not find in their native places. Low income dispassionately motivated them to migrate. Thus, it is clear that economic backwardness influenced these poor women to migrate to urban areas for want of alternative employment, where they also could find a regular minimum wage/ income for their sustenance. Economic factors like better livelihood, higher wages and income, better living conditions, best use of skills, unemployment have caused people to reside in the city.

Occupational Status of Migrants before Migration to the Study Area

Occupational background of the respondents is an important factor influencing the decision to migrate or to stay at their native places. Table 5.2 indicates the details relating to the occupation prior to their migration. Of the 300 sample households, only133 reported that they were migrants and out of these migrants 37 per cent of them worked as agricultural labourers, about a quarter of them worked as non- agricultural labourers and 20 per cent were unemployed. About 13 per cent of them were artisans and the remaining were engaged as domestic servants etc. Among the petty traders' category 61 per cent of them were unemployed before migration, 28 per cent of them were artisans and 11 per cent were non-agricultural labourers. In case of vendors 47 per cent used to work as agricultural labour 29 per cent worked as non-agricultural labourers, 18 per cent were unemployed and another six per cent worked as artisans at their native places.

Table 5.2: Migrants' Occupation before Migration

	Previous/Present Occupation					
	Agricultural Labour	*Non-Agricultural Labour*	*Artisans*	*Un-employed*	*Others*	*Total*
Petty Traders	—	2 (11.11)	5 (27.78)	11 (61.11)	—	18 (100.00)
Vendors	8 (47.00)	5 (29.00)	1 (6.00)	3 (18.00)	—	17 (100.00)
Self-employed	2 (11.11)	4 (22.23)	3 (16.66)	8 (44.44)	1 (5.56)	18 (100.00)
Casual labour	14 (29.78)	21 (44.68)	6 (12.77)	6 (12.77)	—	47 (100.00)
Domestic labour	22 (88.00)	2 (8.00)	1 (4.00)	—	—	25 (100.00)
Salaried workers	3 (37.50)	—	1 (12.50)	—	4 (50.00)	8 (100.00)
Total	49 (36.80)	34 (25.50)	17 (12.70)	28 (21.00)	5 (4.00)	133 (100.00)

Note: Figures in parentheses indicate percentages to total numbers.

In the self employed category, the maximum constituting 44 per cent of them were jobless, 22 per cent worked as non-agricultural labourers, 17 per cent were artisans and the remaining worked in different jobs. In case of casual labourers 45 per cent were non-agricultural labourers, and the remaining worked as agricultural labourers, artisans and were engaged in other jobs. In the domestic labourers' category almost all of them worked as agricultural labourers, whereas in the salaried workers' category, 50 per cent of them were engaged in other works like collecting flowers and selling them to the shops and some of them were engaged in tuitions and 38 per cent of them worked as agricultural labourers and 13 per cent were artisans.

Reasons for Migration

When the reasons for the in-migration of the respondents were elicited, they narrated a wide range of reasons. They can be broadly divided into the following four categories and details are presented in Table 5.3, viz (a) to clear past debts (b) to accompany the family (c) lack of work at the native place and (d) to get better employment.

Table 5. 3: Reasons for Migration

Reasons Occupation	*To clear past debts*	*To accompany the family*	*Lack of work at the native place*	*To have better employment opportunities*	*Total*
Petty Traders	—	3 (16.67)	9 (50.00)	6 (33.33)	18 (100.00)
Vendors	10 (58.83)	2 (11.76)	3 (17.65)	2 (11.76)	17 (100.00)
Self-employed	3 (16.67)	4 (22.23)	5 (27.77)	6 (33.33)	18 (100.00)
Casual labour	5 (10.64)	4 (8.51)	11 (23.40)	27 (57.45)	47 (100.00)
Domestic labour	7 (28.00)	4 (16.00)	10 (40.00)	4 (16.00)	25 (100.00)
Salaried workers	2 (25.00)	4 (50.00)	2 (25.00)	—	8 (100.00)
Total	27 (20.30)	21 (15.79)	40 (30.07)	45 (33.84)	133 (100.00)

Note: Figures in parentheses indicate percentages to total numbers.

The Table shows the reasons, across the selected categories also. As many as 1/3rd of the respondents entered the city life to have better employment opportunities, another 30 per cent migrated for lack of work at their native places. About 20 per cent of them migrated to clear their past debts and the rest of them migrated to accompany their family members. Across the selected categories, in petty traders' category 50 per cent of them migrated for lack of work, 1/3rd migrated to have better employment opportunities and the remaining to accompany the family. In case of vendors the maximum (59%) migrated to clear their past debts. In the self- employed workers' category, 1/3rd of them migrated to have better employment opportunities, while others stated that they migrated for lack of work at their native places, to accompany the family and to clear their past debts. In casual labourers' category, almost all of them migrated to have better employment opportunities and the remaining migrated for other reasons. In the domestic labourers' category 40 per cent of them migrated for lack of work at their native places, and 28 per cent migrated to clear past debts. And in the salaried workers' category, 50 per cent of them migrated to accompany the family. It is interesting to note that none of the respondents has reported that Visakhapatnam City has not attracted them for in-migration. Many of the studies have stated that city attracts in-migration. See for instance, Majumdar[26] who has listed attraction of the city life as one of the reasons for the in-migration.

Place from which Migrated

Information was elicited from the respondents as to indicate their native places within the District or outside the District and the details are presented in Table 5.4.

Table 5. 4: Place from which the respondents Migrated

Occupation	*Places*		
	Within the District	*Outside the District*	*Total*
Petty Traders	12 (66.66)	6 (33.34)	18 (100.00)
Vendors	10 (58.83)	7 (41.17)	17 (100.00)
Self employed	14 (77.78)	4 (22.22)	18 (100.00)
CasualLabour	32 (68.08)	15 (31.92)	47 (100.00)
DomesticLabour	15 (60.00)	10 (40.00)	25 (100.00)
SalariedWorkers	6 (75.00)	2 (25.00)	8 (100.00)
Total	89 (66.92)	44 (33.08)	133 (100.00)

Note: Figures in parentheses indicate percentages to total numbers.

As many as 67 per cent of the respondents migrated from villages within the District. Across the selected categories, 67 per cent petty traders, 59 per cent of vendors', 78 per cent of self employed 68 per cent of casual labourers' 60 per cent of domestic labourers' 75 per cent of salaried workers' migrated from within the District. It is interesting to note that these salaried workers migrated to the city to seek employment as sales girls and to work in fancy stores as they were educated up to secondary level. Further 41 per cent of the respondents from the vendors' category migrated from outside the District due to lack of marketing facilities at their villages and also low demand for their products.

Average Monthly Income of Migrants and Non-Migrants

Average monthly income of the migrants and non-migrants is shown in Table 5.5. It is inferred from this Table that average monthly income of the non migrants is better when compared to the migrants. It is to be expected that the non migrants earn more than the migrants because they belong to the same place and are used to the conditions of labour market and hence may be able to earn better than migrants. Entry into labour market is normally difficult for new comers (migrants) and usually the entry route into labour market for migrants is through friends, relatives and intermediaries.

Table 5.5: Average Monthly Income of Migrants and Non-migrants

Income (Rs)

(1) *Occupation*	*(2)* *Migrants(Rs)*	*(3)* *Non-migrants(Rs)*
Petty Traders	3312.22	3464.37
Vendors	2947.23	3119.06
Self-employed	2692.77	3132.85
Casual labour	2845.53	2876.66
Domestic labour	2173.0	—
Salaried workers	2962.5	3200
Average	2781.63	3189.69

The average monthly income of these 133 migrant respondents was Rs 2782 and average monthly income of the non migrants was Rs 3190. Across the categories petty traders reported an average income of Rs 3312 for migrants and that of non-migrants was Rs 3464. In case of vendors, the average monthly income of the migrants was Rs 2947 and that of the non migrants was Rs 3119. In case of the self employed average monthly income of the migrants was Rs 2693 and that of the non migrants was Rs 3133. In case of the casual labour the average income of the migrants was Rs 2846 and average monthly income of non-migrants was Rs 2877. Domestic labour reported an average monthly income of Rs 2173 for migrants. Among salaried workers' category the average monthly income of the migrants was Rs 2963 and that of the non migrants was Rs 3200. It shows that there is no significant differences between the migrants and the non-migrants.

Summary

While summing up, it has been observed that in petty traders' category 50 per cent of them migrated for seeking work opportunities, 1/3rd migrated to have better employment opportunities and the remaining to accompany their families. From the domestic labourers' category, 40 per cent of them migrated for lack of work at their native places, and 28 per cent migrated to clear past debts. In the salaried workers' category 50 per cent of them migrated to accompany their families.

In case of vendors 59 per cent of them migrated from within the District. A more of less similar picture emerges from the self-employed, casual labourers, domestic labourers. The average monthly income of the 133 migrant respondents was Rs 2782 and that of the non-migrants was Rs 3190. Petty traders' reported an average monthly income of Rs 3312 for migrants and that of non-migrants was Rs 3464. Self-employed category reported an average monthly income of Rs 2693 for migrants and that of the non-migrants was Rs 3133. In case of casual labourers the figures were Rs 2846 and Rs 2877. For domestic labourers the figures were Rs 2173. Among salaried workers' category the figures were Rs 2963 and that of Rs 3200. It shows that there is no significant differences between the migrants and non migrants. The preceding analysis, thus, revealed that migration positively influenced incomes of the migrants.

NOTES

1. Donald. J.B. (1979), "A Migrant's Eye view of the Costs and Benefits of Migration of a Metropolis" In: Alan Brown and Egon Newberger (ed) *Internal Migration Comparative Perspective*, Academic Press, New York, London, p. 68.
2. Thomas, D.S (1993), "Research Memorandum on Migration Differentials", *Social Science Research Bulletin*, New York, p. 4.

3 Theodore. (1954), *The Sociology of Work*, The University of Minnesota Press, Minneapolis, p. 60.

4. Everett Lee (1975), "A Theory of Migration" In: Kenneth C.W. Kammeyer (ed) *Population Studies selected Essay and Research*, Rand McNally College Publishing Company, Chicago, p.191.

5. Peterson. W (1958), "A General Typology of Migration" *Asian Sociological Review*, p. 23-256.

6. Helen I.S. and Brain M.D (1975), *Migration and Development*, Mouton Publishers, the Hauge, p. 1.

7. Beijer, G (1965), " Demographic, Social and Economic Aspects of Internal Migration in some European Countries", United Nations World Population Congress, Belgrade. p.190.

8. Jansen J.C (1954), " Some Sociological Aspects of Migration " in Ajackson (Ed), *Migration*, Cambridge University Press, p. 6010.

9. Keneth Kamneyer, (1975): *Population Studies,* Selected Essays and Research Chicago, p.175.

10. Webster. *Third New International Dictionary*, Mar sealers G. 8c Marsions Co Vol-III, p. 1432.

11. *Multilingual Demographic Dictionary*, United Nations, St/ SoA/ SER Population Studies, New York, Vol. No 29, p. 46. (1956)

12. Chauhan D.S. (1966), *Trends of Urbanisation*, Allied Publishers, New Delhi, p. 85.

13. Upreti. H.C (1981): *Social Organisation of Migration Group*, Himalaya Publishing House, Bombay p.1.

14. Unnithan, J.N.K. *et al.* (ed) (1965): *Towards a Sociology Culture in India*, New Delhi, Prentice Hall.

15. Smith Lynn " Classification and Problems of Migration" In: Wanger and Marevin W.Miksell (ed), *Readings in Cultural Geography,* The University of Chicago Press.

16. Kingsley, D. *Human Society*. The Macmillan Company, New York, 1954, p. 588.

17. Zachariah, K.C (1961) *A Historical Study of Internal Migration in the Indian Subcontinent 1901-31*. Asia Publishing House, pp. 250-51.

18. Peterson *op.cit,* 1958, pp. 23, 49-50.

19. *Census of India*. Migration Tables, 1981.

20. Tara Kumari (1999), *Women in Urban India*, Chugh Publications Allahlabad, pp. 82-83.

21. Kingsley, *op. cit.*

22. Majumdar, D.N (1960): *Social Contours of an Industrial City*, Asia Publishing House, Bombay

23. Dhekney, B.R. (1959): *Hubli City: A Study in Urban Economic Life*, Karnataka University, Dharwar.

24. Theador Caplow (1954): *The Sociology of Work.* The University of Minnosta Press, Minneopolis, p. 60.

6

INCOME, SAVINGS AND CONSUMPTION PATTERN OF THE SAMPLE HOUSEHOLDS

Introduction

This chapter furnishes an analysis of the income, savings and consumption pattern of the selected women respondents across the selected categories and their levels of living based on selected indicators.

Investment Pattern of the Selected Women

As the study relates to the women respondents in the informal sector engaged in different economic activities, an attempt is made at the first instance to examine the investment pattern, sources of investment, etc. Table 6.1 shows the overall investment pattern of all the selected households. Investment pattern has been arranged in intervals from less than Rs. 200 to above Rs. 1200. It is observed that in petty traders' category, 18 per cent of the respondents are investing in between Rs. 200 and Rs. 500 per week for their business dealings, 46 per cent of them are investing in between Rs. 500 and Rs. 800 per week and 36 per cent of them are investing Rs. 800 to Rs. 1200 per week. In case of vendors, 33 per cent of the respondents are able to invest in between Rs. 200 and Rs. 500 per week, 29 per cent of them are investing in between Rs. 500 and Rs. 800 per week, while 26 per cent of them are investing in between Rs. 800 and Rs. 1200 per week. The remaining respondents are scattered around other ranges of investment. A relatively higher proportion of the respondents in the petty traders' category are able to invest between Rs. 500 and Rs. 1200 per week because of the nature of their business activity. For the other categories,

Table 6.1: Investment Pattern of the Selected Women

Investment (Rs)

Occupation	*Nil*	*Less than 200*	*200-500*	*500-800*	*800-1200*	*1200& above*	*Total*
Petty Traders	–	–	9 (46.00)	23 (36.00)	18 (18.00)	–	50 (100.00)
Vendors	10 (8.00)	1 (0.80)	41 (32.80)	36 (28.80)	32 (25.60)	5 (4.00)	125 (100.00)
Self-employed	25 (100.00)	–	–	–	–	–	25 (100.00)
Casual labour	50 (100.00)	–	–	–	–	–	50 (100.00)
Domestic labour	25 (100.00)	–	–	–	–	–	25 (100.00)
Salaried Workers	25 (100.00)	–	–	–	–	–	25 (100.00)
Total	135 (45.00)	1 (0.34)	50 (16.67)	59 (19.66)	50 (16.67)	5 (1.66)	300 (100.00)

Note: Figures in parentheses indicate percentages to total numbers

Table-6.2: Investment Pattern of the Selected Petty Traders and Vendors (Per week)

Occupation	Investment (Rs)						
	Nil	*Less than 200*	*200-500*	*500-800*	*800-1100*	*1200 & above*	*Total*
Petty Traders	—	—	9 (18.00)	23 (46.00)	18 (36.00)	—	50 (100.00)
Vegetable Vendors	—	—	8 (16.00)	12 (24.00)	27 (54.00)	3 (6.00)	50 (100.00)
Fruit Vendors	—	—	5 (20.00)	14 (56.00)	4 (16.00)	2 (8.00)	25 (100.00)
Fish Vendors	10 (20.00)	1 (2.00)	28 (56.00)	10 (20.00)	1 (2.00)	—	50 (100.00)
Total	10 (5.71)	1 (0.57)	50 (28.57)	59 (33.72)	50 (28.57)	5(2.86)	175 (100.00)

Note: Figures in parentheses indicate percentages to total numbers

the investment is nil because they are the wage earners and monthly salaried workers. As such, investment pattern of sample households was analysed for 175 only.

Investment Pattern of the Selected Petty Traders and Vendors (Per week)

As only petty traders and vendors have invested in the business, the pattern of investment, source of investment and other details are elicited only from them and the analysis was confined only to these categories. The analysis is further extended in respect of women vendors as vegetables, fruit and fish vendors. The details are presented in Table 6.2. Across the subdivision of the vendors' category, it is further observed that 54 per cent of women vegetable vendors had invested in between Rs 800 and Rs 1200 per week, while 56 per cent of fruit vendors and 46 per cent of petty traders' had invested Rs. 500 to Rs. 800 per week. On the other hand, 56 per cent of fish vendors invested Rs. 200 to Rs. 500 per week to operate their business , 20 per cent of the respondents from fish vending category worked in fish cutting job and their investment is negligible.

Sources of Investment of the Selected Petty Traders and Vendors

As the respondents are engaged in informal economic activities and mostly belong to socially and economically weaker sections, it is essential to examine the source of investment. The information on the sources of investment of these respondents is furnished in Table 6.3

Table 6.3: Source of Investment of the Selected Petty Traders and Vendors

Occupation	*Source*		
	Own	*Borrowed*	*Total*
Petty traders	1 (2.00)	49 (98.00)	50 (100.00)
Vegetable vendors	–	50 (100.00)	50 (100.00)
Fruit vendors	3 (12.00)	22 (88.00)	25 (100.00)
Fish vendors	4 (8.00)	46 (92.00)	50 (100.00)
Total	8 (4.60)	167 (95.40)	175 (100.00)

Note: Figures in parentheses indicate percentages to total numbers

It may be observed that out of 175 respondents, 167 constituting 95 per cent of them borrowed from non-financial institutions to meet operating expenses, whereas only five per cent of them reported that they are able to manage their business with their own savings. Among different categories, all of the vegetable vendors, 92 per cent of the fish vendors, 88 per cent of the fruit vendors and 98 per cent from petty traders are depending on the non-financial institutions for their business transactions. When asked about sources of borrowing, 95 per cent of the respondents reported to have borrowed from private or small chit funds, private financial agencies, (non- banking finance companies), relatives, friends and money lenders. In addition, it can be seen that mutual dependence of women in informal sector largely rests upon non-financial or non-institutional sources. In spite of heavy interest rates charged by non-financial institutions, still people working in unorganised sector depend on them because of lack of collateral securities and lack of proper knowledge of bank dealings.

Sources of Borrowed Amounts by the Petty Traders and Vendors

Table 6.4 shows the sources of amount borrowed by the petty traders and vendors. Out of the total 167 respondents, 53 per cent of them borrowed these amounts for their business purposes from NBFCs. While, 24 per cent borrowed these amounts from relatives, 15 per cent of them borrowed from friends and 8 per cent of them borrowed from moneylenders. It is distressing to note that a negligible proportion of them have borrowed from institutional sources. Lack of provision of collateral securities and easy and informal ways of transaction have made the respondents to approach the non-institutional agencies despite high interest rates.

Range of Interest Rate paid by the Petty Traders and Vendors

It is clearly evident that most of the respondents rely heavily on non-institutional financial agencies to meet their working capital requirements and none of them has access to institutional financial agencies. This may result in high cost of

Table 6.4: Sources of Borrowed Amounts by the Petty Traders and Vendors

Occupation	Sources					Total
	Finance	*Relatives*	*Friends*	*Moneylenders*	*Bank*	
Petty Traders	31 (63.26)	13 (26.54)	5 (10.20)	—	—	49 (100.00)
VegetablesVendors	20 (40.00)	11 (22.00)	8 (16.00)	10 (20.00)	1 (2.00)	50 (100.00)
Fruit vendors	9 (40.90)	7 (31.82)	3 (13.64)	3 (13.64)	—	22 (100.00)
Fish vendors	28 (60.00)	9 (19.56)	9 (19.56)	—	—	46 (100.00)
Total	88 (52.69)	40 (23.96)	25 (14.98)	13 (7.78)	1 (0.59)	167 (100.00)

Note: Figures in parentheses indicate percentages to total numbers

borrowing, i.e., higher interest rates. To examine this, the interest rates paid by the sample respondents are shown in Table 6.5. The interest rates ranges from 12 per cent to 60 per cent per annum. Out of the 167 respondents, who borrowed, 89 constituting 53 per cent have borrowed the amounts at an interest rate of 36 per cent, whereas, 50 respondents constituting 30 per cent of them have borrowed at an interest rate of 24 per cent. Only 19 respondents have borrowed at an interest rate of 60 per cent. It is further observed that the maximum number of respondents from all the categories like petty traders, vegetables vendors and fruit vendors had to borrow the amounts at high interest rates of 36 per cent.

Repayment Pattern of the Petty Traders and Vendors (Per Month)

The economic viability of the activity in which the sample respondents have engaged may, to some extent, reflect in the repayment performance. Table 6.6 brings out the picture about repayment pattern, which is shown in intervals from below 100 to above Rs. 901 per month. The Table indicates that 52 per cent of the respondents are able to repay in between Rs101 and Rs 300. per month whereas, a quarter of them are repaying in between Rs 301 and Rs 500 per month and the remaining of them are scattered unevenly in between other ranges. Further, among all the groups, a relatively higher proportion of fruit vendors (21 per cent) are repaying above Rs 900 per month.

Income Range of the Petty Traders and Vendors (Per week)

After analysing the investment pattern and sources of investment of the selected sample households, an attempt has been made to examine the income earned by the women respondents from the activity in which they are engaged. This is followed by an analysis of income earnings of the other family members to arrive at the total family earnings. The distribution of petty traders and different categories of vendors with regard to the income earned by them is presented in Table- 6.7. It is found that out of 175 respondents, 44 per cent of them earned

Table- 6.5: Range of Interest Rate paid by the Petty Traders and Vendors

Occupation	Rate of Interest					
	12%	*24%*	*36%*	*48%*	*60%*	*Total*
Petty Traders	—	11 (22.45)	31 (62.26)	1 (2.04)	6 (12.25)	49 (100.00)
VegetableVendors	2 (4.00)	21 (42.00)	21 (42.00)	1 (2.00)	5 (10.00)	50 (100.00)
Fruit vendors	3 (13.64)	2 (9.09)	14 (63.63)	–	3 (13.64)	22 (100.00)
Fish Vendors	—	16 (34.78)	23 (50.00)	2 (4.35)	5 (10.87)	46 (100.00)
Total	5(2.99)	50 (29.94)	89 (53.29)	4 (2.40)	19 (11.38)	167 (100.00)

Note: Figures in parentheses indicate percentages to total numbers.

Table-6.6: Repayment Pattern of the Petty Traders and Vendors (Per month) (Rs)

	Interest paid (Rs)						
Occupation	*1-100*	*101-300*	*301-500*	*501-700*	*701-900*	*901-& above*	*Total*
Petty Traders	4 (8.17)	32 (65.30)	9 (18.36)	4 (8.17)	–	–	49 (100.00)
Vegetable vendors	4 (8.34)	27 (56.25)	13 (27.08)	1 (2.08)	1 (2.08)	2 (4.17)	48 (100.00)
Fruit vendors	2 (8.34)	9 (37.50)	5 (20.83)	1 (4.16)	2 (8.34)	5 (20.83)	24 (100.00)
Fish vendors	8 (17.39)	19 (41.30)	13 (28.26)	3 (6.52)	2 (4.35)	1 (2.18)	46 (100.00)
Total	18 (10.78)	87 (52.09)	40 (23.95)	9 (5.38)	5 (3.00)	8 (4.80)	167 (100.00)

Note: Figures in parentheses indicate percentages to total numbers.

Table 6.7: Income Range of the Petty Traders and Vendors (Per week) (Rs)

	Income (Rs)						
Occupation.	*Below-200*	*201-400*	*401-600*	*601-800*	*801-1000*	*1001- & Above*	*Total*
Petty Traders	—	19 (38.00)	31 (62.00)	—	—	—	50 (100.00)
VegetableVendors	—	4 (8.00)	8 (16.00)	25 (50.00)	9 (18.00)	4 (8.00)	50 (100.00)
Fruit Vendors	—	10 (40.00)	6 (24.00)	8 (32.00)	1 (4.00)	—	25 (100.00)
Fish vendors	—	44 (88.00)	5 (10.00)	1 (2.00)			50 (100.00)
Total	—	77 (44.00)	50 (28.57)	34 (19.43)	10 (5.72)	4 (2.28)	175 (100.00)

Note: Figures in parentheses indicate percentages to total numbers.

in between Rs 201 and Rs 400 per week, 29 per cent earned between Rs 401 and Rs 600 per week and 19 per cent of them earned in between Rs 601 and Rs 800 per week. Only 6 per cent of them were able to earn Rs 801 to Rs 1000 per week and 2 per cent earned above Rs 1001 per week. Across the selected categories, 50 per cent of the vegetable vendors are able to earn in the range of Rs 601 to Rs 800 per week, whereas a higher proportion of fruit vendors (40 per cent) and fish vendors (88 per cent) earned between Rs 201 and Rs 400 per week. On the other hand, about 62 per cent of the petty traders earned between Rs 401 and Rs 600 per week and the rest are unevenly scattered in other ranges.

Average Income of the Petty Traders and Vendors

Table 6.8 indicates the average daily net income of the petty traders and vendors. It is found that average daily net income of the petty traders was Rs 110 whereas, that of vegetable vendors was Rs.97 per day. The vegetable vendors have expressed that their incomes have increased due to abolition of middlemen and establishing *rhythu bazaars*. They felt that they are now able to sell their produce directly to the consumers, which has raised their income levels. The fruit vendors earned Rs 69 per day, due to fluctuations in their business as availability of fruits is seasonal and they are highly

Table 6.8: Average Income of the Petty Traders and Vendors (Rs)

Occupation	*Income (Rs)*			
	Monthly Income	*Monthly Expenditure*	*Monthly Net Income*	*Daily Net Income*
Petty Traders	23098	19794	3304	110
Vegetable Vendors	26570	23670	2900	97
Fruit vendors	21810	19740	2070	69
Fish Vendors	10239	9000	1239	41
Total	20232	17810	2422	81

perishable and for lack of warehousing facilities, they had to sell their product, sometimes at cheaper prices. The fish vendors earned Rs 41 per day, because of supply disturbances and for rough climatic conditions in the sea.

Average Income of the Self-employed Women

Average incomes of the self- employed respondents are presented in Table 6.9. Income is ranged in intervals from Rs 1000 to above Rs 4000. It is found that out of the total 25 respondents, 44 per cent of them earn Rs 2001 to Rs 3000, 40 per cent of them earn between Rs 3001 and Rs 4000 and the remaining earn in between Rs 1000 and Rs 2000 per month. Almost all the women in this field are either skilled or semi skilled and earn better than others compared to other unskilled workers. Further, the literacy levels of this category of respondents are also higher compared to other categories. As indicated earlier, most of the self-employed women are engaged in activities like tailoring and Kirana/Pan Shops.

Table 6.9: Average Income of the Self-Employment Women ranged in intervals (Rs)

	Income (Rs)	
Ranged in intervals	*No. of Self -employed*	*Average income*
1000-1500	2 (8.00)	1200
1500-2000	2 (8.00)	1800
2001-3000	11 (44.00)	2686.36
3001-4000	10 (40.00)	3845
Total	25 (100.00)	2382.84

Note: Figures in parentheses indicate percentages to total numbers.

Average Income of the Casual Labourers

Average income of the casual labourers is shown in Table 6.9. Average income is shown in intervals from Rs 600 to Rs 2000 per month. It is found that 66 per cent of them earn between Rs 1001 and Rs 1400 per month, 24 per cent of them earn from Rs 600 to Rs 1000 per month. The remaining earned between Rs 1401 and Rs 2000 per month. Women engaged in casual labourers' category are mostly illiterates and unskilled compared to the self-employed and earn quite less than the skilled workers. Many respondents in this category are unskilled casual labour like carrying head loads of bricks, sand, cement sacks etc.

Table 6.10: Average Income of the Casual Labourers ranged in intervals (Rs)

Occupation	*Income (Rs)*	
	No. of Casual labourers	*Average income*
600-1000	12 (24.00)	895.83
1001-1400	33 (66.00)	1271.23
1401-1800	3 (6.00)	1536.67
1801-2000	2 (4.00)	2000
Total	50 (100.00)	1425.93

Note: Figures in parentheses indicate percentages to total numbers.

Average Income of the Domestic Labourers

Average incomes of the domestic labourers are shown in intervals from Rs 300 and Rs 1200 per month. It is observed that 44 per cent of them earn between Rs 300 and Rs 500 per month as they are domestic servants and hardly work for 4 to 6 hours per day in one or two houses to supplement their income for the sake of the family (Table 6.11). About 28 per cent of

Table 6.11: Average Income of the Domestic Labourers ranged in intervals (Rs)

Ranged in intervals	*Income*	
	Number of domestic labourers	*Average Income (Rs)*
300-500	11 (44.00)	395.45
501-700	7 (28.00)	850
701-1000	5 (20.00)	930
1001-1200	2 (8.00)	1200
Total	25 (100.00)	843.86

Note: Figures in paretheses indicate percentages to total numbers.

them earn between Rs 501 and Rs 700 per month, 20 per cent of them earn in between Rs 701 and Rs 1000 per month and rest of them earn from Rs 1001 to 1200 per month. In this category, almost all are migrants and illiterates and settled in the city to seek employment.

Average Income of the Salaried Workers

Average incomes of the salaried workers are shown in intervals from Rs 700 and Rs 1500 per month and the details are furnished in the Table 6.12. It is found that 48 per cent of them earn between Rs 1301 and Rs 1500 per month, 36 per cent of them earned between Rs 901 and Rs 1100 per month, and the remaining are scattered in other ranges of income. Salaried workers work in fancy shops, departmental stores, etc as sales girls and work for monthly income to supplement their income for their families. Mostly unmarried girls work as sales girls as they are educated and have the intention to supplement their families in financial matters.

Table 6.12: Average Income of the Salaried Workers ranged in intervals (Rs)

Ranged in interval (Rs.)	*No. of salaried workers*	*Average income (Rs)*
700-900	2 (8.00)	750.00
901-1100	9 (36.00)	1000.00
1101-1300	2 (8.00)	1200.00
1301-1500	12 (48.00)	1500.00
Total	25 (100.00)	1112.50

Note: Figures in parentheses indicate percentages to total numbers.

Income Range of other Family Members (Per Month)

In addition to the sample women respondents, some of the family members are engaged in different economic activities and an analysis is carried out with regard to their earnings. Table 6.13 shows the income ranges of the other members in the family. Majority of them, constituting 61 per cent of them, earned Rs 1,000 to Rs 2,00 per month, whereas 28 per cent of

Table- 6.13: Income Range of Other Family Members (Per Month Rs)

Occupation	Income (Rs)							
	No other Earnings	Below-1000	1001-2000	2001-3000	3001-4000	4001-5000	5001 Above	Total
Petty Traders	1 (2.00)	—	38 (76.00)	11 (22.00)	—	—	—	50 (100.00)
Vendors	17 (13.60)	2 (1.60)	70 (56.00)	27 (21.60)	5 (4.00)	2 (1.60	2 (1.60)	125 (100.00)
Self-employed	4 (16.00)	—	10 (40.00)	11 (44.00)	—	—	—	25 (100.00)
Casual Labour	2 (4.00)	—	33 (66.00)	15 (30.00)	—	—	—	50 (100.00)
Domestic labour	—	—	24 (96.00)	1 (4.00)	—	—	—	25 (100.00)
Salaried Workers	—	—	7(28.00)	18 (72.00)	—	—	—	25 (100.00)
Total	24 (8.00)	2 (0.67)	182 (60.67)	83 (27.67)	5 (1.67)	2 (0.66)	2 (0.66)	300 (100.00)

Note: Figures in parentheses indicate percentages to total numbers

them, earned Rs 2,000 to Rs 3,000 per month, while the remaining are distributed in other ranges.

Across the selected categories, a higher proportion of other family members of petty traders', vendors', casual labourers', and domestic labourers' categories have earned in between Rs 1,000 and Rs 2,000 per month. On the other hand a higher proportion of other family members belonging to self-employed and salaried workers' categories earned Rs 2,000 to Rs 3,000 per month.

Range of Family Gross Income Per Month

Taking into consideration, the average monthly earnings of the sample women respondents and of the other family members, the average gross earnings per month are computed and the details are depicted in Table 6.14. The average ranges are taken into consideration from Rs 1000 to Rs 5000. As many as 123 respondents, constituting 41 per cent, are able to earn nearly Rs 2000 to Rs 3000 per month. Of these, a majority of them are from vendors' category, followed by the casual labourers' and the domestic labourers' categories and the remaining are from other categories. Similarly, another 119 of them (40 per cent) are in the income range of Rs 3000 to Rs 4000 per month and a majority are from vendors' category, followed by the petty traders', casual labourers' categories and the remaining are unevenly scattered in the other ranges.

Annual Income of the Sample Respondents

Table 6.15 furnishes the annual income of the sample respondents presented in income intervals from less then Rs 15,000 to above Rs 65,000. It is evident that out of the 300 sample respondents, the annual income of 60 per cent of respondents was in between Rs 25,001 and Rs 40,000, while 21 per cent of them earned in between Rs 40,000 and Rs 50,000 per annum. The remaining are scattered in other ranges of income. It is further observed that a majority of them earned in between Rs 25,001 and Rs 40,000 per annum. This pattern of income distribution among the respondents indicated that

Table 6.14: Range of Family Gross Income per month (Rs)

	Income (Rs)					
Occupation	*1000-2000*	*2000-3000*	*3000-4000*	*4000-5000*	*5000 & above*	*Total*
Petty Traders	—	7 (14.00)	33 (66.00)	10 (20.00)	—	50 (100.00)
Vendors	14 (11.20)	53 (42.40)	36 (28.80)	15 (12.00)	7 (5.60)	125 (100.00)
Self-Employed	4 (16.00)	10 (40.00)	11 (44.00)	—	—	25 (100.00)
Casual labour	1 (2.00)	29 (58.00)	20 (40.00)	—	—	50 (100.00)
Domestic Labour	6 (24.00)	18 (72.00)	1 (4.00)	—	—	25 (100.00)
Salaried Worker	1 (4.00)	6 (24.00)	18 (72.00)	—	—	25 (100.00)
Total	26 (8.70)	123 (41.00)	119 (39.70)	25 (8.30)	7 (2.30)	300 (100.00)

Note: Figures in parentheses indicate percentages to total numbers

the level of poverty is higher among domestic labourers and it is the lowest among petty traders.

Debt Pattern of the Sample Households

In the preceding sections, the pattern of borrowings is analysed as a source of investment in the economic activity in which they are engaged. That analysis is confined to only two categories, viz, petty traders and vendors. However, the sample respondents have borrowed money to meet different family requirements. Hence, an analysis has been carried out with regard to the amount of debt, interest rate on borrowings, purpose of borrowing etc. A substantial proportion of women working in the unorganised sector (80 per cent) fall in a manageable debt conditions in spite of a fourfold increase in their family income. This is due to the fact that they borrowed the needed capital mostly for the unproductive activities.

Extent of annual debt pattern is shown in Table 6.16. The debt pattern of the respondents ranged in intervals from Rs 500 to Rs 1,00,000. It is observed that a majority of the respondents, constituting 85 per cent, have a debt of Rs 500 to Rs 20,000, whereas 11 per cent of them have an outstanding in between Rs 20,000 and Rs 40,000. It is also found that about two per cent each of the respondents from the vendors' and casual labourers' categories have outstanding debts of above Rs 80,000. While vendors and petty traders have borrowed exclusively for their business operations, the rest of them have borrowed for their domestic needs. Among all categories, about 15 per cent of them have not borrowed any amount and they are continuing their activities pooling own savings. The proportion of non-borrower respondents is found to be relatively higher in domestic labourers' category (20%) followed by casual labourers' (12%) and vendors (8%). Almost all the self employed and salaried workers have borrowed.

Sources of Borrowing of the Sample Households

The sample households have borrowed from both institutional and non–institutional sources. However, the proportion of respondents borrowing from institutional agencies

Table 6.15: Annual Income of the Sample Respondents:

Occupation	*Income(Rs)*						
	Less than 15,000	*15,001-25,000*	*25,001-40,000*	*40,001-50,000*	*50,001-65000*	*65,000& above*	*Total*
Petty Traders	—	—	26 (52.00)	20 (40.00)	4 (8.00)	—	50 (100.00)
Vendors	—	10 (8.00)	71 (56.80)	22 (17.60)	15 (12.00)	7 (5.60)	125 (100.00)
Self-Employed	2(8.00)	2 (8.00)	16 (64.00)	5 (20.00)	—	—	25 (100.00)
Casual Labour	—	3 (6.00)	42 (84.00)	5 (10.00)	—	—	50 (100.00)
Domestic Labour	—	12 (48.00)	13 (52.00)	—	—	—	25 (100.00)
Salaried Workers	—	1 (4.00)	12 (48.00)	12 (48.00)	—	—	25 (100.00)
Total	2(0.67)	28 (9.34)	180 (60.00)	64 (21.33)	19 (6.33)	7 (2.33)	300 (100.00)

Note: Figures in parentheses indicate percentages to total numbers

Table 6.16: Extent of Annual Family Debt Pattern of the Respondents

Occupation	*Annual Debt (Rs)*						*Total*
	500-20,000	*20,000-40,000*	*40,000-60,000*	*60,000-80,000*	*80,000-100000*	*100000& above*	
Petty Traders	44 (89.79)	5 (10.21)	—	—	—	—	49 (100.00)
Vendors	85 (72.04)	24 (20.34)	3 (2.54)	4 (3.38)	2 (1.70)	—	118 (100.00)
Self-employed	23 (92.00)	2 (8.00)	—	—	—	—	25 (100.00)
Casual Labour	42 (95.46)	1 (2.27)	—	—	—	1 (2.27)	44 (100.00)
Domestic labour	20 (100.00)	—	—	—	—	—	20 (100.00)
Salaried workers	25 (100.00)	—	—	—	—	—	25 (100.00)
Total	239 (85.05)	32 (11.38)	3 (1.07)	4 (1.43)	2 (0.72)	1 (0.35)	281 (100.00)

Note: Figures in parentheses indicate percentages to total numbers

Table 6.17: Source of Borrowing of the Sample households

Occupation	Sources					
	Finance	*Relatives*	*Friends*	*Moneylenders*	*Bank*	*Total*
Petty Traders	31 (63.26)	13 (26.53)	5 (10.21)	—	—	49 (100.00)
Vendors	57 (48.30)	27 (22.88)	20 (16.95)	13 (11.02)	1(0.85)	118 (100.00)
Self-employed	10 (40.00)	9 (36.00)	5 (20.00)	1 (4.00)	—	25 (100.00)
Casual Labour	19 (43.18)	7 (15.91)	13 (29.55)	5 (11.36)	—	44 (100.00)
Domestic Labour	9 (45.00)	4 (20.00)	2 (10.00)	5 (25.00)	—	20 (100.00)
Salaried workers	11 (44.00)	5 (20.00)	4 (16.00)	5 (20.00)	—	25 (100.00)
Total	137 (48.75)	65 (23.13)	49 (17.44)	29 (10.32)	1 (0.36)	281 (100.00)

Note: Figures in parentheses indicate percentages to total numbers

Table 6.18: Extent, and Source of Borrowing of the Sample Households

Sources	Amount (Rs)						Total
	500-20,000	*20,000-40,000*	*40,000-60,000*	*60,000-80,000*	*80,000-100000*	*100000 & above*	
Finance	109 (79.57)	19 (13.87)	4 (2.92)	3 (2.18)	1 (0.73)	1 (0.73)	137 (48.75)
Relatives	55 (84.62)	7 (10.76)	1 (1.54)	1 (1.54)	1 (1.54)	—	65 (23.13)
Friends	45 (91.84)	4 (8.16)	—	—	—	—	49 (17.44)
Moneylenders	26 (89.65)	3 (10.35)	—	—	—	—	29 (10.33)
Bank	1 (100.00)	—	—	—	—	—	1 (0.35)
Total	236 (83.98)	33 (11.74)	5 (1.78)	4 (1.43)	2 (0.72)	1(0.35)	281 (100.00)

Note: Figures in parentheses indicate percentages to total numbers

is almost negligible and above 99 per cent of the sample respondents are depending on non-institutional sources to meet their credit requirements. The distribution of sample borrower respondents in relation to the source and extent of borrowing is presented in Table 6.17 It is evident that, of the 281 borrower respondents, as high as 49 per cent are depending on NBFCs to meet their credit requirements (Table 6.17). Next to this, relatives appear to be a dominant source by providing credit to 23 per cent of the respondents. This is followed by friends (17%) and moneylenders (10%). Almost the same phenomenon appears among different categories of sample respondents with varying proportions. A significant point to be noted is that, the NBFCs will advance money and they will collect the amounts on a daily basis.

Extent, and Sources of Borrowing of the Sample households

The sources of borrowing and extent of amount taken are shown in Table 6.18. It is observed that out of 281 borrower respondents, 84 per cent have borrowed an amount in the range of Rs 500 to Rs 20,000 and another 12 per cent have borrowed in the range of Rs 20,000 to Rs 40,000. Further, it is also observed that, irrespective of the source of borrowing, a higher proportion have borrowed in the range of Rs.500 to Rs. 20,000. Though, the proportion of borrowers is small, it is only the NBFCs and relatives are advancing higher amounts of above Rs 40,000.

Extent, and Source of Borrowing of the Petty traders

Table 6.19 indicated that in petty traders' category majority (90 per cent) of the respondents have borrowed in between Rs 500 to Rs 20,000 and only 10 per cent of them have borrowed in between the range of Rs 20,000 to Rs 40,000. While 63 per cent of the respondents have approached the NBFCs for credit, 27 per cent of them have borrowed from relatives and 10 per cent of them from friends. As indicated earlier, most of the respondents of this category have migrated to the urban surroundings to perform their business due to financial crisis at their places of origin and as they do not possess collateral securities, they rely heavily on NBFCs for credit.

Table 6.19: Extent, and Source of Borrowing of the Petty Traders

Occupation	*Amount (Rs)* 500-20,000	20,000-40,000	40,000-60,000	60,000-80,000	80,000-100000	Above 100000	*Total*
Finance	28 (90.33)	3 (9.67)	—	—	—	—	31 (63.26)
Relatives	11 (84.62)	2 (15.38)	—	—	—	—	13 (26.54)
Friends	5 (100.00)	—	—	—	—	—	5 (10.20)
Moneylenders	—	—	—	—	—	—	—
Bank	—	—	—	—	—	—	—
Total	44 (89.79)	5 (10.21)	—	—	—	—	49 (100.00)

Note: Figures in brackets indicate percentages to total numbers

Table- 6.20: Extent, and Source of borrowing of the Vendors

	Amount (Rs)						
Occupation	*500-20,000*	*20,000-40,000*	*40,000-60,000*	*60,000-80,000*	*80,000-100000*	*Above-100000*	*Total*
Finance	37 (64.92)	14 (24.56)	2 (3.51)	3 (5.26)	1 (1.75)	—	65 (48.31)
Relatives	21 (77.78)	3 (11.12)	1 (3.70)	1 (3.70)	1 (3.70)	—	27 (22.88)
Friends	15 (75.00)	5 (25.00)	—	—	—	—	20 (16.95)
Moneylenders	11 (84.62)	2 (15.38)					13 (11.02)
Bank	1 (100.00)						1 (0.84)
Total	85 (72.04)	24 (20.34)	3 (2.54)	4 (3.39)	2 (1.69)	—	118 (100.00)

Note: Figures in brackets indicate percentages to total numbers

Table 6.21: Extent, and Source of borrowing of the Self -Employed

Occupation	*Amount (Rs)* 500-20,000	*20,000-40,000*	*40,000-60,000*	*60,000-80,000*	*80,000-100000*	*Above-100000*	*Total*
Finance	8 (80.00)	2 (20.00)	—	—	—	—	10 (40.00)
Relatives	9 (100.00)	—	—	—	—	—	9 (36.00)
Friends	5 (100.00)	—	—	—	—	—	5 (20.00)
Moneylenders	1 (100.00)	—	—	—	—	—	1 (4.00)
Bank	—	—	—	—	—	—	—
Total	23(92.00	2(8.00)	—	—	—	—	25 (100.00)

Note: Figures in parentheses indicate percentages to total numbers

Extent, and Source of Borrowing of the Vendors

With regard to vendors it is observed that 72 per cent of the respondents have borrowed in the range of Rs 500 to Rs 20,000, 20 per cent of them have borrowed in the range of Rs 20,000 to Rs. 40,000,three per cent each of them have borrowed in between Rs. 60,000 to Rs 80,000, and in between Rs 40,000 to Rs.60,000,two per cent of the respondents have borrowed in between Rs 80,000 to Rs 100000. Further, it is evident that 48 per cent of the respondents have borrowed from NBFCs, 23 per cent of them from relatives, 17 per cent from friends, 11 per cent from moneylenders and only 0.84 per cent of the respondents have borrowed from institutional sources.

Extent, and Source of Borrowing of the Self-Employed

Table 6.21 shows that almost all the self-employed respondents have borrowed an amount of Rs. 500 to Rs. 20,000. In this category, 40 per cent of them have borrowed from NBFCs, 36 per cent from relatives and rest of them from friends and moneylenders. In this self-employed category, almost all of them are migrants who entered the city for employment, and borrowed to purchase sewing machines to supplement their family incomes.

Extent, and Source of Borrowing of the Casual Labour

Table 6.22 indicates that in casual labours' category almost all of them have borrowed in between Rs. 500 to Rs 20,000. Among different sources, about 43 per cent of them have borrowed from NBFCs, followed by friends (30%), relatives (16%) and moneylenders (11%). A majority of them have no skills and their earnings are lower than the skilled persons. Low income and lack of collateral securities have forced them to borrow from non-institutional agencies.

Extent, and Source of borrowing of the Domestic Labour

According to Table 6.22 in domestic labourers' category all the respondents have borrowed in between the range of Rs 500 to Rs 20,000. As 36 per cent of them borrowed from NBFCs, 20 per cent of them have borrowed from moneylenders, 16 per

Table 6.22: Extent, and Source of borrowing of the Casual Labour

Occupation	Amount (Rs) 500-20,000	20,000-40,000	40,000-60,000	60,000-80,000	80,000-100000	Above-100000	Total
Finance	18 (94.74)	—	—	—	—	1 (5.26)	19 (43.18)
Relatives	7 (100.00)	—	—	—	—	—	7 (15.91)
Friends	13 (100.00)	—	—	—	—	—	13 (29.55)
Moneylenders	4 (80.00)	1 (20.00)	—	—	—	—	5 (11.36)
Bank	—	—	—	—	—	—	—
Total	42 (95.46)	1 (2.27)	—	—	—	1 (2.27)	44 (100.00)

Note: Figures in parentheses indicate percentages to total numbers

Table- 6.23: Extent, and Source of borrowing of the Domestic Labour

Occupation	Amount (Rs)						Total
	500-20,000	*20,000-40,000*	*40,000-60,000*	*60,000-80,000*	*80,000-100000*	*Above-100000*	
Finance	9 (100.00)	—	—	—	—	—	9 (36.00)
Relatives	4 (100.00)	—	—	—	—	—	4 (16.00)
Friends	2 (100.00)	—	—	—	—	—	2 (8.00)
Moneylenders	5 (100.00)	—	—	—	—	—	5 (20.00)
Bank	—	—	—	—	—	—	—
Total	25 (100.00)	—	—	—	—	—	25 (100.00)

Note: Figures in parentheses indicate percentages to total numbers

Table 6.24: Extent, and Source of Borrowing of the Salaried Workers

Occupation	*Amount (Rs)*						
	500-20,000	*20,000-40,000*	*40,000-60,000*	*60,000-80,000*	*80,000-100000*	*Above-100000*	*Total*
Finance	11 (100.00)	—	—	—	—	—	11 (44.00)
Relatives	5 (100.00)	—	—	—	—	—	5 (20.00)
Friends	4 (100.00)	—	—	—	—	—	4 (16.00)
Moneylenders	5 (100.00)	—	—	—	—	—	5 (20.00)
Total	25 (100.00)	—	—	—	—	—	25 (100.00)

Note: Figures in parenheses indicate percentages to total numbers

cent of them from relatives and 8 per cent of them borrowed from friends. Though income levels of the domestic labourers are quite low, still some of them are depending on moneylenders in spite of high interest rates charged by them. Almost all of them are migrants and borrowed amounts to settle in the City and also to meet the family consumption requirements.

Extent, and Source of Borrowing of the Salaried Workers

Table 6.24 indicated that in salaried worker' category, all of the respondents have borrowed in between Rs 500 and Rs 20,000. Whereas 44 per cent of them have borrowed the credit from NBFCs, rest of them have borrowed from other sources i.e., relatives (20%), friends (16%) and moneylenders (20%). Large size of the family and high dependency ratio has forced them to borrow to maintain their basic necessities of the family.

Interest Rates paid by the Borrowers

It is evident that the sample respondents do not have the access to the institutional financial agencies and they are depending on non- institutional sources to meet their credit requirements, where in the interest rates are generally high. To examine this aspect, the distribution of the respondents with regard to the interest rates at which they borrowed is shown in Table 6.25. It is found that out of 281 respondents, the maximum of 139, constituting 49 per cent, borrowed at an exorbitant interest rate of 36 per cent, followed by 37 per cent of borrowers with interest rate of 24 per cent. Across the selected categories, 63 per cent of the petty traders, 48 per cent of vendors and 70 per cent of domestic labourers borrowed at the interest rate of 36 per cent, whereas,59 per cent of casual labourers,48 per cent of self-employed, 34 per cent of vendors and 32 per cent of salaried workers borrowed at the interest rate of 24 per cent and the remaining are scattered in other ranges.

Purpose and Extent of Borrowings

Borrowing for consumption purpose indicates poverty, while for income generation indicates low resource - base of a family. It may be observed from the Table 6.26, that of the 300 sample households 281 respondents have borrowed capital for

Table -6.25: Interest Rates paid by the Borrowers

Occupation	Interest Rate(Rs) 12%	24%	36%	48%	60%	Total
Petty Traders	—	11 (22.45)	31 (63.26)	1 (2.04)	6 (12.25)	49 (100.00)
Vendors	5 (4.24)	40 (33.90)	57 (48.30)	3 (2.54)	13 (11.02)	118 (100.00)
Self-employed	1 (4.00)	12(48.00)	12 (48.00)			25 (100.00)
Casual Labour	1 (2.27	26 (59.09)	17 (38.64)	—	—	44 (100.00)
Domestic Labour	—	6 (30.00)	14 (70.00)	—	—	20 (100.00)
Salaried Workers	—	8 (32.00)	8 (32.00)	—	9 (36.00)	25 (100.00)
Total	7 (2.50)	103 (36.33)	139 (49.46)	4 (1.42)	28 (9.96)	281 (100.00)

Note: Figures in parentheses indicate percentages to total numbers

different reasons. Of the borrower respondents as high, as 38 per cent have borrowed for consumption purposes and 36 per cent of them borrowed to meet their business expenses. Another 13 per cent of them reported that they have taken the amount for medical expenses, nine per cent have borrowed for house construction and repairs and five per cent borrowed capital for performing marriages and for religious ceremonies. It is observed that more than one-half of the respondents have borrowed in between Rs 500 and Rs 20,000 for consumption, business expenditure, medical expenses and for house construction. Moreover, 11 per cent of the respondents borrowed the amount in between Rs 20,000 and Rs 40,000 mostly for marriages and ceremonies. A very few respondents have borrowed above Rs 1,00,000 mainly for house construction.

The foregoing analysis presents details on purpose and extent of borrowing category- wise. Among different categories, it is evident from Table 6.27, that 84 per cent of the respondents from petty traders' category have borrowed for business expenses and 12 per cent for consumption purpose, four per cent of them borrowed for house construction. Among vendors' category, 47 per cent of them have borrowed the amount for business expenses, 20 per cent of them borrowed for consumption and the remaining for other purposes. (Table 6.28) When self- employed category is considered, about 70 per cent of the respondents have borrowed amounts for business expenses like purchasing sewing machine, followed by 22 per cent for house construction and 9 per cent for consumption expenses (Table 6.29). About 61 per cent of the respondents from casual labourers' category have borrowed the amount for consumption purpose due to low income, followed by 23 per cent for house construction, 9 per cent for medical expenses and 7 per cent for marriages and religious ceremonies (Table 6.30). (Table 6.31) indicated that in domestic labourers' category, 75 per cent of them have borrowed the amount for consumption purposes due to low income, followed by 25 per cent for house construction. As high as 84 per cent of the salaried worker respondents have reported that their borrowings are meant for meeting family consumption expenditure (Table 6.32) and this

Table -6.26: Purpose and Extent of Borrowings

Purpose	*Amount(Rs)* 500-20,000	20,000-40,000	40,000-60,000	60,000-80,000	80,000-100000	Above-100000	*Total*
Business Expenses	84 (84.00)	15 (15.00)	—	1 (1.00)	—	—	100 (35.58)
ConsumptionExpenditure	103 (96.26)	3 (2.80)	1 (0.94)	—	—	—	107 (38.08)
Expenditure onMarriage& Ceremonies	3 (21.43)	8 (57.15)	1 (7.14)	1 (7.14)	1 (7.14)	—	14 (4.98)
Medical Expenses	31 (86.12)	4 (11.11)	—	—	1 (2.77)	—	36 (12.82)
House construction	18 (75.00)	2 (8.34)	1 (4.16)	2 (8.34)	—	1 (4.16)	24 (8.54)
Total	239 (85.05)	32 (11.38)	3 (1.06)	4 (1.43)	2(0.72)	1 (0.36)	281 (100.00)

Note: Figures in parentheses indicate percentages to total numbers

Table -6.27: Purpose and Extent of Borrowings of Petty Traders

Purpose	Amount(Rs)						Total
	500-20,000	20,000-40,000	40,000-60,000	60,000-80,000	80,000-100000	Above-100000	
Business Expenses	36 (87.00)	5 (12.20)	—	—	—	—	41 (83.67)
ConsumptionExpenditure	6 (12.00)	—	—	—	—	—	6 (12.25)
Expenditure onMarriage& Ceremonies	—	—	—	—	—	—	—
Medical Expenses	—	—	—	—	—	—	—
House construction	2	—	—	—	—	—	2 (4.08)
Total	44 (89.79)	5 (10.21)	—	—	—	—	49 (100.00)

Note: Figures in parentheses indicate percentages to total numbers

Table 6.28: Purpose and Extent of Borrowings of Vendors

Purpose	*Amount (Rs)*					
	500-20,000	*20,000-40,000*	*40,000-60,000*	*60,000-80,000*	*80,000-100000*	*Total*
Business Expenses	47 (83.93)	8 (14.28)	—	1 (1.78)	—	56 (47.46)
Consumption Expenditure	19 (79.16)	4 (16.67)	1 (4.17)	—	—	24 (20.34)
Expenditure on Marriage& Ceremonies	10 (71.43)	1 (7.14)	1 (7.14)	2 (14.28)	—	14 (11.86)
Medical Expenses	2 (15.39)	8 (61.54)	1 (7.69)	1 (7.69)	1 (7.69)	13 (11.02)
House construction	7 (63.64)	3 (27.27)	—	—	1 (9.09)	11 (9.32)
Total	85 (72.04)	24 (20.34)	3 (2.54)	4 (3.38)	2 (1.70)	118 (100.00)

Note: Figures in parentheses indicate percentages to total numbers

Table 6.29 Purpose and Extent of Borrowings of Self-employed

Purpose	*Amount (Rs)*					*Total*
	500-20,000	*20,000-40,000*	*40,000-60,000*	*60,000-80,000*	*80,000-100000*	
Business Expenses	16 (69.56)	—	—	—	—	16 (69.56)
Consumption Expenditure	2 (8.70)	—	—	—	—	2 (8.70)
Expenditure on Marriage& Ceremonies	—	—	—	—	—	—
Medical Expenses	5 (21.74)	—	—	—	—	5 (21.74)
House construction	—	—	—	—	—	—
Total	23 (100.00)	—	—	—	—	23 (100.00)

Note: Figures in parentheses indicate percentages to total numbers

Table 6.30: Purpose and Extent of Borrowings of Casual Labour

Purpose	Amount (Rs)						
	500-20,000	*20,000-40,000*	*40,000-60,000*	*60,000-80,000*	*80,000-100000*	*Above 100000*	*Total*
Business Expenses	—	—	—	—	—	—	—
Consumption Expenditure	26(96.30)	—	—	—	—	1(3.70)	27(61.36)
Expenditure on Marriage & Ceremonies	1(33.33)	1(33.33)	—	—	—	1(33.33)	3(6.82)
Medical Expenses	—	—	4(8.0)	—	—	—	4(9.09)
House construction	10(20.00)	—	—	—	—	—	10(22.73)
Total	37(84.09)	1(2.27)	4(9.09)	—	—	2(4.55)	44(100.00)

Note: Figures inparentheses indicate percentages to total numbers

Table 6.31: Purpose and Extent of Borrowings of Domestic Labour

Purpose	*Amount (Rs)*						*Total*
	500-20,000	*20,000-40,000*	*40,000-60,000*	*60,000-80,000*	*80,000-100000*	*Above 100000*	
Business Expenses	—	—	—	—	—	—	—
Consumption Expenditure	15 (75.00)	—	—	—	—	—	15 (75.00)
Expenditure on Marriage & Ceremonies	—	—	—	—	—	—	—
Medical Expenses	—	—	—	—	—	—	—
House construction	5 (25.00)	—	—	—	—	—	5 (25.00)
Total	20 (100.00)	—	—	—	—	—	20 (100.00)

Note: Figures in parentheses indicate percentages to total numbers

Table 6.32: Purpose and Extent of Borrowing of Salaried Workers

Purpose	*Amount (Rs)*						
	500-20,000	*20,000-40,000*	*40,000-60,000*	*60,000-80,000*	*80,000-100000*	*Above-100000*	*Total*
Business Expenses	–	–	–	–	–	–	–
Consumption Expenditure	21 (84.00)	–	–	–	–	–	–
Expenditure on Marriage & Ceremonies	3 (12.00)	–	–	–	–	–	–
Medical Expenses	–	–	–	–	–	–	–
House construction	1 (4.00)	–	–	–	–	–	–
Total	25 (100.00)	–	–	–	–	–	–

Note: Figures in parentheses parentheses percentages to total numbers.

Table 6.33: Purpose of Borrowing of the Sample Households

Occupation	*Purpose*					*Total*
	Business Expenses	*Consumption Expenditure*	*Expenditure on marriage & ceremonies*	*Medical Expenses*	*House Construction*	
Petty Traders	41 (83.67)	6 (12.25)	—	—	2 (4.08)	49(100.00)
Vendors	56 (47.46)	24 (20.34)	14 (11.86)	13(11.02)	11 (9.32)	118(100.00)
Self-employed	2 (8.00)	16 (64.00)	2 (8.00)	—	5 (20.00)	25(100.00)
Casual labour	—	27 (61.36)	3 (6.82)	1(2.27)	13 (29.55)	44(100.00)
Domestic labour	—	15 (75.00)	—	—	5 (25.00)	20(100.00)
Salaried Workers	—	21 (84.00)	3 (12.00)	—	1 (4.00)	25(100.00)
Total	99 (35.23)	109 (38.79)	22 (7.83)	14 (4.98)	37 (13.17)	281(100.00)

Note: Figures in parentheses indicate percentages to total numbers

is followed by expenditure on social and religious ceremonies (12 %) and house construction expenditure (4%).

Purpose of Borrowing of the Sample households

Table 6.33 shows the purpose of borrowing of the sample households. It is to be observed that out of the total 281 borrower respondents, 109 of them constituting 39 per cent have borrowed for the consumption expenses, followed by business expenses (35percent) house construction and repairs (13%) and the remaining of the respondents borrowed for religious ceremonies, marriages and for medical expenses. Across the selected categories 84 per cent of the respondents from petty traders' category, 47 per cent from vendors' categories had borrowed mainly for business expenses. On the other hand, majority of the respondents from self-employed, casual labourers', domestic labourers' and salaried workers' categories have borrowed for consumption expenses. Insufficient income from the economic activity in which they engaged might have forced these respondents to borrow for consumption purpose also.

Savings Pattern

Savings is one of the important indicators to depict the standard of living. Table 6.34 shows the picture of savings

Table 6.34: Savings Pattern

	Savings(Rs)		
Occupation	*Yes*	*No*	*Total*
Petty traders	34 (68.00)	16 (32.00)	50 (100.00)
Vendors	96 (76.80)	29 (23.20)	125 (100.00)
Self-employed	22 (88.00)	3 (12.00)	25 (100.00)
Casual Labour	43 (86.00)	7 (14.00)	50 (100.00)
Domestic labour	21 (84.00)	4 (16.00)	25 (100.00)
Salaried Workers	15 (60.00)	10 (40.00)	25 (100.00)
Total	231 (77.00)	69 (23.00)	300 (100.00)

Note: Figures in parentheses indicate percentages to total numbers

pattern of the sample households. It is observed from the Table that out of the total sample of 300 households, 231, constituting 77 per cent, of the respondents, have the intention to save whereas the rest constituting 23 per cent of the sample households are not able to save any part of their earnings. A majority of the respondents across all the categories have the motive to save, while a few of them have no intention to save due to low income, and are not able to meet both the ends. Most of them are single earners in the family.

Monthly Family Savings

Table 6.35 indicates the saving pattern of the sample households. It is gratifying to note that the maximum number 231 women have expressed their motive to save and that is shown in ranges. It is further observed from the Table that a majority of these households, which constitutes 48 per cent, are saving in between Rs 150 to Rs 300 per month, while 37 per cent of them are able to save upto Rs 150 per month from their earnings. Across the selected categories, petty traders, vendors, and salaried workers are able to save Rs 150 to Rs 300 per month, whereas self employed, casual labourers and domestic labourers are able to save only below Rs 150 per month. The remaining households are unevenly scattered in other ranges. It can be further observed from the Table that the maximum (40%) of the respondents from salaried workers'

Table 6.35: Monthly Family Savings (Rs)

	Saving (Rs)				
Occupation	*Below-150*	*150-300*	*300-600*	*600& above*	*Total*
Petty Traders	10 (29.41)	21 (61.76)	3 (8.83)	—	34 (100.00)
Vendors	28 (29.17)	49 (51.04)	18 (18.75)	1 (1.04)	96 (100.00)
Self-employed	14 (63.64)	6 (27.27)	2 (9.09)	—	22 (100.00)
Casual Labour	20 (46.52)	18 (41.86)	5 (11.62)	—	43 (100.00)
Domestic Labour	10 (47.62)	9 (42.85)	2 (9.53)	—	21 (100.00)
Salaried workers	3 (20.00)	8 (53.34)	4 (26.66)	—	15 (100.00)
Total	85(36.80)	111(48.05)	34(14.72)	1(0.43)	231(100.00)

Note: Figures in parentheses indicate percentages to total numbers

category have no ability to save from their earnings because of their high dependency ratio and large family size, which obstructs their intentions to save.

Place of Savings of the Sample Households

Table 6.36 indicates that out of 231 respondents, 32 per cent have saved their earnings in private chit funds, followed by 29 per cent with their friends, 24 per cent with co-operative banks/post office, 12 per cent of them retained the savings with themselves, and only 3 per cent of them saved their earnings with their employers. Across the selected categories, 44 per cent of petty traders have saved their earnings with their friends, 38 per cent from vendors' and 30 per cent of casual labourers' categories have saved their earnings in cooperative bank/post office, 32 per cent of the self-employed and 40 per cent of salaried workers had kept their savings in private chit funds, 38 per cent of domestic labour kept their savings with friends.

Consumption Pattern of the Sample Households

Eventhough income, savings and investment broadly indicate the economic status of the sample households, it would be more appropriate to study the consumption pattern, which is a direct indicator to present the levels of living of the sample households. The consumption patterns had been studied with reference to three broad categories viz Food items, Non-Food items and expenditure on addictive habits.

Consumption Pattern on Food Items

Table 6.37 indicates the annual per captia food consumption of the sample households and eight major food items were taken into consideration, viz cereals, pulses, edible oils, vegetables, milk, non vegetarian items like fish, chicken, mutton and eggs, sugar tea and others. It is found from the Table that, on an average the per capita annual expenditure on food items worked out to Rs 3929 and of this expenditure, about 40 per cent is spent on consuming cereals. This is followed by expenditure on non-vegetarian items (16%), vegetables (14%), milk (9%) and edible oils (7%). Across the selected

Table 6.36: Places of Savings of the Sample Households

Occupation	Place of Savings (Rs)					Total
	With the employer	*With Friends*	*With co-operative bank / post office*	*Private chit fund*	*With themselves*	
Petty Traders	15 (44.12)	5 (14.70)	11 (32.35)	3 (8.83)	34 (100.00)	
Vendors	—	25 (26.05)	29 (30.20)	36 (37.50)	6 (6.25)	96 (100.00)
Self-Employed	—	6 (27.27)	3 (13.64)	7 (31.82)	6 (27.27)	22 (100.00)
CasualLabour	5 (11.63)	10 (23.25)	13 (30.23)	8 (18.61)	7 (16.28)	43 (100.00)
Domestic Labour	2 (9.53)	8 (38.09)	4 (19.05)	5 (23.80)	2 (9.53)	21 (100.00)
Salaried Workers	—	4 (26.66)	2 (13.34)	6 (40.00)	3 (20.00)	15 (100.00)
Total	7(3.03)	65(29.44)	56(24.24)	73(31.61)	27 (11.68)	231 (100.00)

Note: Figures in parentheses indicate percentages to total numbers

Table 6.37: Occupation Wise Annual per Capita Food Consumption:

Occupation	Annual per Capita consumption								
	Cereals	*Pulses*	*Edible oil*	*Vegetables*	*Milk*	*Non-vegetarian*	*Sugar/tea*	*Others*	*Total*
Petty traders	1915.26 (43.63)	168.24 (3.83)	280.00 (6.38)	672.9 (15.33)	488.7 (11.13)	541.44 (12.33)	125.16 (2.85)	198.6 (4.52)	4390.3 (100.00)
Vendors	1534.18 (39.70)	150.47 (3.90)	269.48 (6.98)	498.14 (12.88)	258.42 (6.68)	641.96 (16.60)	86.71 (2.24)	425.87 (11.02)	3865.23 (100.00)
Self-employed	1343.06 (35.20)	144.13 (3.80)	248.13 (6.50)	623.3 (16.40)	318.00 (8.40)	673.33 (17.70)	117.33 (3.00)	345.33 (9.00)	3812.61 (100.00)
Casual labour	1458.52 (38.04)	171.08 (4.46)	225.02 (5.87)	597.08 (15.57)	363.90 (9.50)	669.96 (17.47)	105.37 (2.75)	243.20 (6.34)	3834.1 (100.00)
Domestic Labour	1284.56 (37.77)	117.88 (3.46)	206.25 (6.07)	508.23 (14.94)	337.41 (9.92)	647.71 (19.04)	95.29 (2.80)	204.14 (6.00)	3401.47 (100.00)
Salaried Workers	1704.96 (41.00)	158.89 (3.82)	256.5 (6.16)	608.03 (14.62)	401.78 (9.65)	683.03 (16.43)	126.42 (3.04)	219.64 (5.28)	4159.25 (100.00)
Total	1562.59 (39.77)	154.32 (3.93)	255.69 (6.51)	564.19 (14.36)	337.87 (8.60)	636.39 (16.20)	102.80 (2.62)	315.17 (8.01)	3929.02 (100.00)

Note: Figures in parentheses indicate percentages to total *numbers*

Table 6.38: Occupation wise Annual Per Capita Non-food Consumption

Occupation	*Annual per Capita Non-Food Consumption*								
	Clothing	*Housing*	*Fuel*	*Medical Expenses*	*Electri-city*	*Entertain-ment*	*Education*	*Others*	*Total*
Petty Traders	389.0 (6.13)	1776.32 (28.00)	840.0 (13.24)	65.1 (1.03)	660.6 (10.41)	295.8 (4.67)	874.2 (13.78)	1443.0 (22.74)	6344.02 (100.00)
Vendors	443.4 (12.17)	1165.03 (32.00)	551.0 (15.13)	141.0 (3.87)	426.5 (11.71)	267.7 (7.35)	224.0 (6.15)	423.2 (11. 62)	3641.83 (100.00)
Self-employed	434.5 (9.55)	2114.04 (46.46)	538.0 (11.82)	122.7 (2.70)	344.0 (7.56)	484.0 (10.63)	248.7 (5.46)	264.0 (5.80)	4549.94 (100.00)
Casual labour	390.3 (11.42)	1572.82 (46.03)	455.0 (13.31)	114.5 (3.35)	300.6 (8.80)	244.7 (7.16)	154.7 (4.53)	184.0 (5. 40)	3416.62 (100.00)
Domestic Labour	314.1 (9.27)	1596.26 (47.10)	522.4 (15.42)	105.9 (3.13)	296.5 (8.75)	204.0 (6.02)	163.0 (4.81)	186.4 (5.50)	3388.56 (100.00)
Salaried Workers	390.2 (9.84)	1635. 84 (41. 34)	732. 8 (18. 52)	74. 0 (1.87)	391.6 (9. 89)	323.6 (8. 18)	275.4 (6. 96)	134.0 (3.40)	3957.44 (100.00)
Total	409.53 (9.90)	1489.13 (36.01)	594.85 (14.38)	113.90 (2.76)	423.92 (10.25)	285.92 (6.91)	322.08 (7.79)	496.20 (12.00)	4135.53 (100.00)

categories, the per capita annual consumption expenditure is the highest in petty traders' (Rs 4390) and the lowest in domestic labourers' (Rs 3400) categories. With regard to the relative position of different items of the food basket across the categories, a more or less similar pattern is depicted in the overall position though with varying proportions.

Consumption Pattern on Non-food Items

The proportion of expenditure on non-food items is significant in their consumption expenditure. Eight items are considered viz clothing, housing, fuel, medical expenses, electricity, entertainment, education, and others. On an average, the per capita annual expenditure on non- food items worked out to Rs 4154 (Table 6.38) and it is found to be about 6 per cent higher than the per capita annual expenditure on food items. Across different categories, this expenditure is the highest in petty traders' (Rs. 6344) and the lowest in domestic labourers' (Rs 3383) categories. Further, expenditure on housing, i.e., house rent alone constitute about 36 per cent, followed by expenditure on fuel (14%) clothing (10%), electricity (10%), education (8%) and entertainment (7%). A similar pattern with varying proportions is discernable among different categories also.

Pattern of Expenditure on Addictive Habits

There are certain addictive habits in the society like chewing tobacco and consuming liquor. The annual per captia expenditure on addictive habits of the sample households is shown in Table 6.39. It is evident that the per capita annual expenditure on addictive items worked out to Rs 328 or less than one rupee per day. Of this expenditure, about 48 per cent is spent on tobacco and the remaining on liquor. Across different categories, this expenditure is the highest in domestic labourers' (Rs 486) and the lowest in petty traders' (Rs 76) categories. It is also evident, that the relative expenditure on consumption of liquor and social status are inversely related.

Table 6.39: Annual Per Capita Expenditure on Addictive Habits by the Sample Households

	Addictive Habits		
Occupation	*Tobacco*	*Liquor & others*	*Total*
Petty Traders	55. 0 (72.40)	21.00 (27.60)	76.00 (100.00)
Vendors	194.20 (48.40)	206.8 (51.60)	401.00 (100.00)
Self-Employed	76.00 (38.80)	120.0 (61.20)	196.00 (100.30)
Casual Labour	180.3 (51.80)	167.80 (48.20)	348.10 (100.30)
Domestic labour	220.2 (45.30)	265.40 (54.60)	485.60 (100.50)
Salaried Workers	142.5 (36.0)	252.80 (64.00)	395.30 (100.80)
Total	156.69 (47.84)	170.82 (52.16)	327.51 (100.00)

Note: Figures in brackets indicate percentages to total numbers

Annual Expenditure of the Sample households

Table 6.40 indicates the annual expenditure of the sample households. A majority of the sample households constituting 52 per cent of them are spending in the range of Rs 3000 and Rs 4000 per month, while others are scattered unevenly in other ranges. Across the selected categories, a majority of the vendors, self-employed, and casual labour spends in between Rs 2000 and Rs 3000 per month, whereas others are spending nearly around Rs 4000 per month. A majority of the sample households from domestic labourers' category are spending nearly about Rs 2000 per month.

Status of Dwelling

Patten or status of dwelling is considered as one of the important indicators to measure the quality of life of a family. Therefore, it would be useful to study the problems of housing and other facilities to understand living conditions of the urban women working in informal sector.

Type of Dwelling

The dwelling houses of the sample women are classified into the following three categories

Table 6.40: Annual Expenditure of the Sample Households

Occupation	*Expenditure (Rs)*						
	Less than 15,000	*15,001-25,000*	*25,001-40,000*	*40,001-50,000*	*50,001-65,000*	*65,00& Above*	*Total*
Petty Traders	—	—	26 (52.00)	23 (46.00)	1 (2.00)	—	50 (100.00)
Vendors	1 (0.8)	30 (24.0)	72 (57.6)	15 (12.0)	6 (4.8)	1(0.8)	125(100.00)
Self-employed	1 (4.00)	4 (16.00)	18 (72.00)	2 (8.00)	—	—	25 (100.00)
Casual Labour	—	10 (20.00)	40 (80.00)	—	—	—	50 (100.00)
Domestic Labour	—	15 (60.00)	10 (40.00)	—	—	—	25 (100.00)
Salaried Workers	—	1 (4.00)	17 (68.00)	7 (28.00)	—	—	25 (100.00)
Total	2 (0.67)	60 (20.00)	183 (61.00)	47 (15.67)	7 (2.33)	1 (0.33)	300(100.00)

Note: Figures in parentheses indicate percentages to total numbers

- Type I (*Pucca* house)
- Type II (Semi-*pucca* house)
- Type III (*kutcha* house)

It is to be noted that respondents staying in Type I (*pucca* houses) are considered better situated than the other categories and those respondents staying in Type II, (semi-*pucca* houses) are considered better than Type III, (*kutcha* house). The information regarding dwelling type shows that 46 per cent of the respondents are residing in Type III houses, followed by 33 per cent staying in Type II houses and 21 per cent residing in Type I houses (Table 6.41).

Table 6.41: Type of Dwelling

Occupation	*Type of Dwelling*			*Total*
	Pucca Type I	*Kutcha Type III*	*Semi-pucca Type II*	
Petty Traders	8 (16.00)	9 (18.00)	33 (66.00)	50 (100.00)
Vendors	34 (27.20)	59 (47.20)	32 (25. 60)	125 (100.00)
Self-employed	10 (40.00)	5 (20.00)	10 (40.00)	25 (100.00)
Casual Labour	7(14.00)	30 (60.00)	13 (26.00)	50 (100.00)
Domestic Labour	5 (20.00)	16 (64.0)	4 (16.00)	25 (100.00)
SalariedWorkers	—	18 (72.00)	7 (28.00)	25 (100.00)
Total	64 (21.34)	137 (45.66)	99 (33.00)	300 (100.00)

Note: Figures in brackets indicate percentages to total numbers

Across the selected categories, a majority (66%) of the respondents from petty traders are residing in Type II houses, followed by 18 per cent in Type III houses. In the vendors' category, 47 per cent of them are staying in Type III houses, followed by 27 per cent in Type I pucca houses. While 40 per cent each in the self-employed category are residing in Type I and Type II, the remaining are residing in Type III houses. More than one-half of the respondents from the casual labourers' category are living in Type III houses, followed by 26 per cent residing in Type II. In the case of domestic labourers' and salaried workers' categories more than per cent of them are staying in Type III dwellings.

Housing Status by Ownership

It can be observed from Table 6.42 that 51 per cent of the respondents are residing in rented accommodation, whereas 48 per cent of them have own houses. It is to be noted that a majority of the respondents from the vendors' category have own houses (constituting 74 per cent) followed by salaried workers (44%) and petty traders (62%) for the simple reason that they are non-migrants. It is also found that their standard of living is a better than other categories. As high as 90 per cent of respondents from casual labourers' category are residing in rented accommodation, followed by domestic labourers' (88%) and self-employed categories (76%).This is because of their low incomes and as they are migrants. On the other hand, 12 per cent of the domestic labourers are neither having their own houses nor staying in rented houses as their husbands are working as security guards in apartments, which provide them a single room tenement for their living.

Table 6.42: Housing status by ownership

	Housing Status			
Occupation	*Own*	*Rented*	*Others*	*Total*
Petty Traders	31 (62.00)	19 (38.00)	—	50 (100.00)
Vendors	92 (73.60)	33 (26.40)	—	125 (100.00)
Self employed	6 (24.00)	19 (76.00)	—	25 (100.00)
Casual Labour	5 (10.00)	45 (90.00)	—	50 (100.00)
Domestic Labour	—	22 (88.00)	3 (12.00)	25 (100.00)
Salaried workers	11 (44.00)	14 (56.00)	—	25 (100.00)
Total	145 (48.33)	152 (50.67)	3 (1.00)	300 (100.00)

Note: Figures in parentheses indicate percentages to total numbers

Type I *Pucca* Dwelling

From Table 6.43 it can be observed that out of 64 pucca houses, about 60 per cent are owned and the remaining are rented. Across the selected categories, 88 per cent of petty traders are residing in their own pucca houses followed by vendors (68%), and self-employed (50%). None of the salaried workers is residing in pucca houses.

Table 6.43: Housing Status-1 (*pucca*)

Occupation	*Housing status*		
	Own	*Rented*	*Total*
Petty Traders	7 (87.50)	1 (12.50)	8 (100.00)
Vendors	23 (67.65)	11 (32.35)	34 (100.00)
Self employed	5 (50.00))	5 (50.00))	10 (100.00)
Casual Labour	1 (14.28)	6 (85.72)	7 (100.00)
Domestic Labour	2 (40.00)	3 (60.00)	5 (100.00)
Salaried Workers	—	—	—
Total	38 (59.37)	26 (40.63)	64 (100.00)

Note: Figures in parentheses indicate percentages to total numbers

Type II Semi-*Pucca* Dwelling

As many as 57 respondents are residing in rented houses and 42 are staying in own semi-pucca houses (Table 6.44). Across the selected categories, 78 per cent of vendors' are having their own semi pucca houses followed by petty traders (49%), and casual labour (2%). In this type of housing, all the sample households belonging to self-employed, domestic labourers' and salaried workers' categories are residing in rented accommodation only.

Table 6.44: Housing Status-II (Semi-*Pucca*)

Occupation	*Housing status*		
	Own	*Rented*	*Total*
Petty Traders	16 (48.48)	17 (51.52)	33 (100.00)
Vendors	25 (78.13)	7 (21.87)	32 (100.00)
Self employed	—	10 (100.00)	10 (100.00)
Casual Labour	1 (7.70)	12 (92.30)	13 (100.00)
Domestic Labour	—	4	4 (100.00)
Salaried Workers	—	7	7 (100.00)
Total	42 (42.43)	57 (57.57)	99 (100.00)

Note: Figures in parentheses indicate percentages to total numbers

Type III *Kutcha* Dwelling

Table 6.45 shows that out of 137 kutcha houses, 51 per cent of the respondents are staying in kutcha rented houses and the remaining are residing in kutcha own houses. Across the selected categories, 89 per cent of petty traders,75 per cent of vendors and 61 per cent of the salaried workers are residing in own houses of this type. Cent per cent of domestic labour are residing in rented houses of this category.

Table 6.45: Housing Status-III (*kutcha*)

Occupation	*Housing status*		
	Own	*Rented*	*Total*
Petty Traders	8 (88.89)	1 (11.11)	9 (100.00)
Vendors	44 (74.57)	15 (25.43)	59 (100.00)
Self employed	1 (20.00))	4 (80.00))	5 (100.00)
Casual Labour	3 (10.00)	27 (90.00))	30 (100.00)
Domestic Labour	—	16 (100.00)	16 (100.00))
Salaried Workers	11 (61.12)	7 (38.88)	18 (100.00)
Total	67 (48.90)	70 (51.10)	137 (100.00)

Note: Figures in parentheses indicate percentages to total numbers

Kitchen Status by use of fuel

It can be observed from Table 6.46 that as many as 53 per cent of women are using LPG as a main source of fuel for cooking, followed by 27 per cent using firewood, two per cent using kerosene and one per cent using both LPG and kerosene for cooking. It is also observed that 97 per cent of petty traders and 68 per cent of self-employed are using LPG as the main fuel for cooking. Another 45 per cent of vendors and 38 per cent of casual labour are using firewood as a medium of fuel. Another 48 per cent of domestic labourers are using both kerosene and firewood for cooking and for almost all the salaried workers LPG is the main fuel for cooking.

Status of electrification of dwelling house

Table 6.47 shows that almost all the houses are electrified,

Table 6.46: Kitchen Status by use of fuel

Used Occupation	*Fuel*						*Total*
	LPG	*Kerosene*	*Firewood*	*LPG & Kerosene*	*LPG & Firewood*	*Kerosene & Firewood*	
Petty Traders	48 (96.00)	1 (2.00)	—	—	—	1 (2.00)	50 (100.00)
Vendors	45 (36.00)	2 (1.60)	56 (44.80)	1 (0.80)	8 (6.40)	13 (10.40)	125 (100.00)
Self-employed	17 (68.00)	1 (4.00)	5 (20.00)	—	—	2 (8.00)	25 (100.00)
Casual Labour	18 (36.00)	1 (2.00)	19 (38.00)	2 (4.00)	—	10 (20.00)	50 (100.00)
Domestic Labour	9 (36.00)	1 (4.00)	—	—	3 (12.00)	12 (48.00)	25 (100.00)
Salaried Workers	23 (92.00)	—	—	—	—	2 (8.00)	25 (100.00)
Total	160 (53.30)	6 (2.00)	80 (26.70)	3 (1.00)	11 (3.70)	40 (13.30)	300 (100.00)

Note: Figures in parentheses indicate percentages to total numbers

whereas, only three per cent of them are living without electricity in their houses. Across the selected categories, a majority of them have electrified their houses. Only 4 per cent in self-employed, eight per cent in the domestic labourers', three per cent in vendors and two per cent in petty traders' categories do not have electricity in their houses.

Table 6.47: Status of Electrification of Dwelling House

Occupation	*Status of power*		*Total*
	Yes	*No*	
Petty traders	49 (98.00)	1 (2.00)	50 (100.00)
Vendors	121 (96.00)	4 (3.20)	125 (100.00)
Self-employed	24 (96.00)	1 (4.00)	25 (100.00)
Casual Labour	50 (100.00)	—	50 (100.00)
Domestic Labour	23 (92.00)	2 (8.00)	25 (100.00)
Salaried workers	25 (100.00)	—	25 (100.00)
Total	292 (97.34)	8 (2.66)	300 (100.00)

Note: Figures in parentheses indicate percentages to total numbers

Protected Water Supply

From Table 6.48, it can be seen that 91 per cent of the respondents have access to protected water supply from public taps, whereas 8 per cent fetch water from public hand pumps. Among the selected categories, almost all the respondents have access to the protected water supply. However, they depend mostly on public sources quite nearer to their settlements but some of them have to fetch it from a distance of one km away from their settlements.

Sanitary Conditions

Table 6.25 furnishes the picture on the sanitary conditions of the respondents. It can be observed that 59 per cent of them have no lavatory facilities in their settlements and they have to depend on public lavatories, whereas 41 per cent of them have lavatories at their settlements. The picture across the selected categories indicates that 76 per cent of vendors, 92 per cent of salaried workers, 78 per cent of casual labour and 64 per cent

Table 6.48: Protected Water Supply

Occupation	Source					Total
	Protected	Well	Hand pump	Protected & well	Protected & hand pump	
PettyTraders	50 (100.00)	—	—	—	—	50 (100.00)
Vendors	120 (96.00)	2 (1.60)	2 (1.60)	1 (0.80)	—	125 (100.00)
Self-employed	25 (100.00)	—	—	—	—	25 (100.00)
CasualLabour	42 (84.00)	—	—	—	8 (16.00)	50 (100.00)
Domestic Labour	10 (40.00)	—	—	—	15 (60.00)	25 (100.00)
SalariedWorkers	25 (100.00)	—	—	—	—	25 (100.00)
Total	272 (90.67)	2 (0.67)	2 (0.67)	1 (0.33)	23 (7.66)	300 (100.00)

Note: Figures in parentheses indicate percentages to total numbers

of domestic labour do not have separate lavatory facilities at their houses. They depend on public toilets. On the other hand, 90 per cent of petty traders, 84 per cent of self-employed, 36 per cent of domestic labour, and 28 per cent of salaried workers have toilet facilities of their own. The settlements do not have separate bathing places and lavatory facilities. The environments of the settlements appear very dirty, dusty and filthy. Presence of liquid wastes in the ditches, and on the road sides, piling up of dust and garbage on the road paths and absence of drainage facilities are leading to environmental pollution and are spreading contagious diseases in the settlements resulting in frequent ill health among the inhabitants.

Table 6.49: Sanitary Conditions

	Sanitary Conditions		
Occupation	*PublicToilets*	*Owntoilets*	*Total*
Petty Traders	5 (10.00)	45 (90.00)	50 (100.00)
Vendors	95 (76.00)	30 (24.00)	125 (100.00)
Self-employed	4 (16.00)	21 (84.00)	25 (100.00)
CasualLabour	39 (78.00)	11 (22.00)	50 (100.00)
Domestic labour	16 (64.00)	9 (36.00)	25 (100.00)
Salaried workers	18 (72.00)	7 (28.00)	25 (100.00)
Total	177 (59.00)	123 (41.00)	300 (100.00)

Note: Figures in parentheses indicate percentages to total numbers

Asset Structure

It is further desirable to examine and analyse the asset structure of the respondents. Table 6.50 brings out this classification with regard to the division. This Table brings out that about 43 per cent of them are having assets in the range of Rs. 5000 and Rs 20000 and 13 per cent of them are having assets in the range of below Rs 5000. The remaining respondents are unevenly scattered in other ranges. This analysis brings out that a majority of the respondents are having low assets, which invites some other helping hand in uplifting their living standards.

Table 6.50: Asset Structure

Occupation	Value of Asset								Total
	Below-500	*5000-20,000*	*20,000-35,000*	*35,000-50,000*	*50,000-65,000*	*65,000-80,000*	*80,000-100000*	*100000-above*	
Petty Traders'	—	19 (38.00)	1 (2.00)	—	2 (4.00)	7 (14.00)	12 (24.00)	9 (18.00)	50 (100.00)
Vendors	11 (8.80)	31 (24.80)	17 (13.60)	16(12.80)	22 (17.60)	11 (8.80)	5 (4.00)	12 (9.60)	125 (100.00)
Self-employed	2 (8.00)	17 (13.60)	—	—	1 (4.00)	1 (4.00)	1 (4.00)	3 (12.00)	25 (100.00)
Casual Labour	15 (30.00)	31 (62.00)	1 (2.00)	—	2 (4.00)	—	1 (2.00)	—	50 (100.00)
Domestic Labour	10 (40.00)	15 (60.00)	—	—	—	—	—	—	25 (100.00)
Salaried Workers	—	15 (60.00)	—	—	5 (20.00)	3(12.00)	1 (4.00)	1(4.00)	25 (100.00)
Total	38 (12.70)	128 (42.70)	19 (6.30)	16 (5.30)	32 (10.70)	22 (7.30)	20 (6.70)	25 (8.30)	300 (100.00)

Note: Figures in parentheses indicate percentages to total numbers

Table 6.51: Expenditure on Recreation

Occupation	*Recreation*							*Total*
	Nil	*Below-100*	*101-150*	*150-200*	*201-250*	*251-300*	*301-Above*	
Petty Traders	16 (32.00)	21 (42.00)	13 (26.00)	—	—	—	—	50 (100.00)
Vendors	31 (24.80)	71 (56.80)	13 (10.40)	3(2.40)	—	1(0.80)	6 (4.80)	125 (100.00)
Self-employed	2 (8.00)	6 (24.00)	9 (36.00)	5(20.00)	2(8.00)	—	1 (4.00)	25 (100.00)
CasualLabour	28 (56.00)	11 (22.00)	10 (20.00)	—	—	—	—	50 (100.00)
DomesticLabour	21 (84.00)	4 (16.00)	—	—	—	—	—	25 (100.00)
SalariedWorkers	—	1 (4.00)	18 (72.00)	5(20.00)	—	—	1 (4.00)	25 (100.00)
Total	99 (33.00)	131 (43.60)	50 (16.60)	8(2.70)	2(0.70)	2(0.70)	8(2.70)	300 (100.00)

Note: Figures in parentheses indicate percentages to total numbers

Table 6.52: Expenditure on Health

Occupation	*Expenditure on health*											*Total*
	Below-1000	*1001-2000*	*2001-3000*	*3001-4000*	*4001-5000*	*5001-6000*	*6001-7000*	*7001-8000*	*8001-9000*	*9001-10,000*	*10,001& above*	
Petty Traders	19	3	—	—	—	—	—	—	—	2	—	24 (11.59)
Vendors	68	11	4	2	3	2	—	—	2	2	7	101 (48.79)
Self-employed	11	3	1	—	—	—	1	—	—	—	1	17 (8.22)
Casual labour	28	4	—	2	2	2	—	—	—	1	—	39 (18.84)
DomesticLabour	10	5	—	—	—	—	—	1	—	—	1	17 (8.22)
SalariedWorkers	9	—	—	—	—	—	—	—	—	—	—	9 (4.34)
Total	145 (70.05)	26 (12.56)	5 (2.42)	4 (1.93)	5 (2.42)	4 (1.93)	1 (0.48)	1 (0.48)	2 (0.96)	5 (2.42)	9 (4.35)	207 (100.00)

Note: Figures in brackets indicate percentages to total numbers

Expenditure incurred on Recreation

Table 6.51, shows that 44 per cent of the respondents are able to spend in the range of Rs 100 to Rs 150 per month on recreation, whereas, 33 per cent of them are spending below Rs 100 per month. Across the selected categories vendors, self-employed and salaried workers are able to spend between Rs 100 and Rs 150 per month on recreation and the rest of them are spending below Rs 100 per month. It is distressing to note that about three per cent of the respondents do not have any means to spend on recreation.

Health Conditions

Preventive and curative health care services are provided free of cost, though inadequately, by the Government. Preventive health care is provided almost freely under mass immunization programmes. It is found that very few respondents along with their family are approaching to public health services being provided by the government.

Table 6.52 shows the expenditure on health by the sample respondents. About 16 per cent of the respondents are spending from Rs 300 to Rs 600 yearly on health and the remaining are scattered unevenly in other ranges of expenditure. About 7 per cent of respondents are spending above Rs 4000 per year on health alone. It has been observed that people working in informal sector mostly suffer from nutrition deficiency and poor health resulting from poor sanitation conditions. Some communicable diseases such as diarrhoea, dysentery, worm-infection, measles, and typhoid are common due to inadequate sanitation facilities and water contamination.

Respiratory ailments like coughs and colds, tuberculosis, diphtheria and pneumonia are commonly found in these areas. Mostly woman face these problems in addition to general weakness, because they have to shoulder a large part of their domestic duties before going to work. It is also seen that they do not generally seek treatment for an ailment until homemade remedies prove futile. They usually approach hospitals, when the disease reaches an acute stage. Further due to ignorance, they do not take in full the course of medication.

Role of Women in Decision Making

The quality of life can be considered from the viewpoint of not only physical indicators but also from other indicators such as their role in decision-making. This information is provided in Table 6.53.

Table 6.53: Role of Women in Decision-making

	Role of Women			
Occupation	*Independent*	*Dependent*	*Cannot say*	*Total*
Petty Traders	—	49 (98.00)	1 (2.00)	50 (100.00)
Vendors	30 (24.00)	55 (44.00)	40 (32.00)	125 (100.00)
Self-employed	6 (24.00)	18 (72.00)	1 (4.00)	25 (100.00)
Casual Labour	3 (6.00)	43 (86.00)	4 (8.0)	50 (100.00)
Domestic Labour	1 (4.00)	24 (96.00)	—	25 (100.00)
Salaried Workers	—	15 (60.00)	10 (40.00)	25 (100.00)
Total	40 (13.34)	204 (68.00)	56 (18.66)	300 (100.00)

Note: Figures in parentheses indicate percentages to total numbers

It shows that 68 per cent of the respondents are still dependent on husband, father or somebody else to take decisions regarding their family matters and 19 per cent of them are not able to say anything about their role in decision making because they are either widows, or divorced and unmarried and they are the bread earners to their family without depending on others. Moreover, 13 per cent of them are independent and they take own decisions regarding their family matters because of the disability of the principal bread earner. It may be observed that in almost all the categories women are depending on their family members for decision-making.

Spouses' Attitude Regarding the Work of Women

It is gratifying to note that 56 per cent of women are encouraged by family members regarding their work. Table 6.54 shows that they get logistical and physical support by their spouses, and another 29 per cent seek satisfactory attitude from their spouses, whereas 15 per cent are not seeking any encouragement because they are the bread earners for their family and re-establishing the family without any help and support of any body-else.

Table 6.54: Spouses' Attitude Towards Women

Occupation	*Attitude*			*Total*
	Encouraging	*Satisfactory*	*None*	
Petty Traders	30 (60.00)	19 (38.00)	1 (2.00)	50 (100.0)
Vendors	78 (62.40)	22 (17.60)	25 (20.00)	125 (100.00)
Self-employed	18 (72.00)	3 (12.00)	4 (16.00)	25 (100.00)
Casual Labour	19 (38.00)	27 (54.00)	4 (8.00)	50 (100.00)
Domestic Work	12 (48.00)	12 (48.00)	1 (4.00)	25 (100.00)
Salaried Workers	10 (40.00)	5 (20.00)	10 (40.00)	25 (100.00)
Total	167 (55.70)	88 (29.30)	45 (15.00)	3000 (100.00)

Note: Figures in parentheses indicate percentages to total numbers

Participation of Women in Welfare Organisations

Table 6.55 shows the participation of women in welfare organisations. It is observed that 73 per cent of them are not participating in welfare organisations due to lack of proper education, lack of time and awareness regarding the organisation and 13 per cent of them are participating in Government welfare organisation like DWCRA groups etc. In addition, 12 per cent of them are participating in private welfare organisation like Spandana.

Table 6.55: Participation of Women in Welfare Organisations

	Welfareorganization				
Occupation	*Government organization*	*Private organization*	*Both 1&2*	*None*	*Total*
Petty Traders	3 (6.00)	—	—	47 (94.00)	50 (100.00)
Vendors	19 (15.0)	26 (20.80)	7 (5.60)	73 (58.40)	125 (100.00)
Self-employed	4 (16.00)	2 (8.00)	—	19 (76.00)	25 (100.00)
Casual labour	11 (22.00)	6 (12.00)	—	33 (66.00)	50 (100.00)
Domestic labour	3 (12.00)	1 (4.00)	—	21 (84.00)	25 (100.00)
Salaried workers	—	—	—	25 (100.00)	25 (100.00)
Total	40 (13.34)	35 (11.66)	7 (2.34)	218 (72.66)	300 (100.00)

Note: Figures in parentheses indicate percentages to total numbers

Reasons for women working in the Informal Sector

Women workers from poor families prefer to work in informal sector and Table 6.56 indicates the strong reasons for their preference.

Table 6.56: Reasons to prefer Work in the Informal Sector

Reasons	*No of respondents*	*%*
Poverty	41	13.66
Lack of higher education	73	24.34
To learn working skills	25	8.34
For Better employment	114	38.00
Others	47	15.66
Total	300	(100.00)

Note: Figures in parentheses indicate percentages to total numbers

About 38 per cent of the women preferred to work in the unorganised sector to seek for employment opportunities, whereas 24 per cent of them joined the unorganised sector due to lack of education, while, others joined the work in informal sector either due to poverty or lack of skills.

Persons Who Guided them to Join the Sector

About 62 per cent of them joined this sector with the guidance of their relatives, whereas 34 per cent of them obtained work in the unorganised sector with the help and support of their friends

Table 6.57: Persons Who Guided them to Join the Sector

Guidance	*No of respondents*	*%*
Friends	101	33.67
Relatives	185	61.67
Others	14	4.66
Total	300	(100.00)

Note: Figures in parentheses indicate percentages to total numbers

Satisfaction regarding their Occupations

Table 6.58 shows that 99 per cent of them are quite satisfied with their occupations, to supplement their income to their family to lead the life with necessities. They are quite happy because they are able to earn for the family even without any education and proper training.

Table 6.58: Satisfaction Regarding their Occupations

Satisfaction	*Number of the respondents*	*%*
Satisfied	297	99.00
Not satisfied	3	1.00
Total	300	(100.00)

Note: Figures in brackets indicate percentages to total numbers

Whereas, only one per cent of the respondents are not satisfied by their work but they have to continue with the same work for lack of financial and logistical support.

Distance between work place and residence

Table 6.59 explains the distance between work place and residence and 50 per cent of the respondents are nearly travelling 1km to 5km from their residence to reach their work places, and 32 per cent of them are working in the vicinity of their houses. Some of them are coming from far off places for their work. It is observed that most of the domestic labour, self-employed and petty traders are travelling from nearby areas, whereas casual labourers, vendors and salaried workers travel far off places to reach their work places

Table 6.59: Distance between work place and residence

Distance between work place and residence	*Number of respondents*	%
Nearby	95	(31.67)
1- 5km	149	(49.67)
6 -10km	27	(9.00)
11 -15km	5	(1.66)
16 - 20km	7	(2.34)
21- 25km	17	(5.66)
Total	300	(100.00)

Note: Figures in parentheses indicate percentages to total numbers

Summary

The major conclusions emerging from the Study are as follows:

The Study revealed that in petty traders' category, 18 per cent of them are investing in between Rs 200 and Rs 500 per week for their business dealings, 46 per cent of them are investing in between Rs 500 and Rs 800 per week and 36 per cent of them are investing Rs. 800 to Rs. 1200 per week. In case of vendors, 33 per cent of them are able to invest in between Rs. 200 and Rs. 500 per week, 29 per cent of them are investing in between Rs.500 and Rs. 800/- per week, whereas 26 per cent of them are investing in between Rs. 800 and Rs. 1200 per week.

Across the sub division of vendors, 54 per cent of women vegetable vendors had invested in between Rs 800 and Rs 1200 per week, while 56 per cent of fruit vendors and 46 per cent of petty traders had invested Rs. 500 to Rs. 800 per week. On the other hand, 56 per cent of fish vendors invested Rs. 200 to Rs. 500 per week to operate their business, 20 per cent of the respondents from fish vending category worked in fish cutting job and their investment is negligible. All the vegetable vendors, 92 of per cent fish vendors, 88 per cent of fruit vendors, almost all petty traders are depending on the NFBCs for their business transactions. While, 224 per cent borrowed these amount from relatives, 15 per cent from friends and 8 per cent from moneylenders. Lack of provision of collateral securities and easy and informal ways of transaction have mode the respondents to approach the NFBCs despite high interest rates. The interest rates ranges from 12 per cent to 60 per cent per annum. Out of the 167 respondents who borrowed, 89 constituting 53 per cent have borrowed at an interest rate of 36 per cent, whereas, 50 respondents constituting 30 per cent of them have borrowed at an interest rate of 24 per cent. Only 19 respondents have borrowed at an interest rate of 60 per cent.

Out of 175 respondent, 44 per cent of them earned in between Rs 201 and Rs 400 per week, 29 per cent earned between Rs 401 and Rs 600 per week and 19 per cent of them earned in between Rs 601 and Rs 800 per week. Only 6 per cent of them were able to earn Rs 801 to Rs 1000 per week and 2 per cent earned above Rs 1001 per week. Across the selected categories, 50 per cent of the vegetable vendors are able to earn in the range of Rs 601 to Rs 800 per week, whereas a higher proportion of fruit vendors (40%) and fish vendors (88%) earned between Rs 201 and Rs 400 per week.

The average income of the self- employed respondents ranged from Rs 1000 to above Rs 4000/-. It is found that out of the total 25 respondents, 44 per cent of them earned Rs 2001 to Rs 3000 40 per cent of them earned between Rs 3001 and Rs

4000 and the remaining earned in between Rs 1000 and Rs2000 per month. Almost all the women in this field are either skilled or semi-skilled and earned better than others compared to other unskilled workers.

Average income is shown in intervals from Rs 600/- to Rs 2000 per month It is found that 66 per cent of them earn between Rs 1001 and Rs 1400 per month, 24 per cent of them earned from Rs 600 to Rs 1000 per month. The remaining earned between Rs 1401 to Rs 2000 per month. Women engaged in casual labourers' category are mostly illiterates and unskilled compared to the self-employed and earned quite less than the skilled workers. Average income of the domestic labourers are shown in intervals from Rs 300 and Rs 1200 per month. It is observed that 44 per cent of them earned between Rs 300 and Rs 500 per month as they are domestic servants and hardly work for 4 to 6 hours per day in one or two houses to supplement their income for the sake of the family. Almost all are migrants and illiterates in this category and settled in the City to seek employment. Average incomes of the salaried workers are shown in intervals from Rs 700 and Rs 1500 per month. It is found that 48 per cent of them earned between Rs 1301 and Rs 1500 per month, 36 per cent of them earned between Rs 901 and Rs 1100 per month, and the remaining are scattered in other ranges of income. Salaried workers worked in fancy shops, departmental stores, etc as sales girls and work for monthly income to supplement their family income. Mostly unmarried girls work as sales girls as they are educated and have the intention to supplement their families in financial matters.

Majority of them, constituting 61 per cent, earned Rs 1,000 to Rs 2,000 per month, whereas 28 per cent of them earned Rs 2,000 to Rs 3,000 per month, while the remaining are distributed in other ranges. A higher proportion of other family members of petty traders', vendors', casual labourers', and domestic labourers' categories have earned in between Rs 1,000 and Rs 2,000 per month. On the other, hand a higher proportion of other family members belonging to self-employed and salaried workers' categories earned Rs 2,000 to Rs 3,000 per month.

The average monthly earnings of the sample respondents and of the other family members, the average gross earnings per month are also computed. The average ranges are taken into consideration from Rs 1000 to Rs 5000. As many as 123 respondents constituting 41 per cent, are able to earn nearly Rs 2000 to Rs 3000 per month. Of these, a majority of them are from vendors' category, followed by casual labourers' and the domestic labourers' categories and the remaining are from other categories. Similarly, another 119 of them (40%) are in the income range of Rs 3000 to Rs 4000 per month and a majority are from vendors' category, followed by the petty traders', casual labourers' categories and the remaining are unevenly scattered in the other ranges

The annual income of 60 per cent of respondents was in between Rs 25,001 and Rs 40,000, while 21 per cent of them earned in between Rs 40,000 and Rs 50,000 per annum. The remaining are scattered in other ranges of income. It is further observed that a majority of them earned in between Rs 25,001 and Rs 40,000 per annum. This pattern of income distribution among, the respondents indicated that the level of poverty is higher among domestic labourers and it is the lowest among petty traders.

The debt pattern of the respondents ranged in intervals from Rs 500 to Rs 1,00,000, 85 per cent have the debt of Rs 500 to Rs 20,000, whereas 11 per cent of them have borrowed in between Rs 20,000 and Rs 40,000. It is also found that about two per cent each of the respondents from the vendors' and casual labourers' categories have borrowed above Rs 80,000. While vendors and petty traders have borrowed exclusively for their business operations, rest of them have borrowed for their domestic needs. Among all categories, about 15 per cent of them have not borrowed any amount and they are continuing their activities pooling own savings. The proportion of non-borrower respondents is found to be relatively higher in domestic labouers category (20%) followed by casual labour (12%) and vendors (8%).

It is observed that out of 281 respondents, 84 per cent have borrowed an amount in the range of Rs 500 and Rs 20,000 and another 12 per cent have borrowed in the range of Rs 20,000 to Rs 40,000. Further, it is also observed that, irrespective of the source of borrowing, a higher proportion have borrowed in the range of Rs 500 and Rs 20,000. Though, the proportion of borrowers is small, it is only the NBFCs and relatives are advancing higher amounts of above Rs 40,000. In petty traders' category, a majority (90 per cent) of them respondent have borrowed in between Rs 500/- to Rs 20,000 and only 10 per cent of them have borrowed in between Rs 20,000 to Rs 40,000. While 63 per cent of the respondents have approached the NBFCs for credit, 27 per cent of them have borrowed from relatives and 10 per cent of them from friends. In vendors' category it is observed that 72 per cent of them have borrowed in the range of Rs 500 to Rs 20,000, 20 per cent of them have borrowed in the range of Rs 20,000 and Rs 40,000, 3 per cent each of them have borrowed in between Rs 60,000 and Rs 80,000, and in between Rs 40,000 and Rs 60,000, 2 per cent of the respondents have borrowed in between Rs 80,000 and Rs 100000. All the respondents from self-employed category have borrowed between Rs 500 and Rs 20,000. While, 44 per cent of them have borrowed from NBFCs, 36 per cent from relatives and rest of them from friends and moneylenders. in casual labourers category almost all of them have borrowed between Rs 500 and Rs 20,000. Among different sources, about 43 per cent of them have borrowed from NBFCs followed by friends (30%), relatives (16%) and moneylenders (11%). In casual labourers category a majority of them have no skills and their earnings are lower than the skilled persons. Low income and lack of collateral securities have forced them to borrow from NFBCs. In domestic labourers category all the respondents have borrowed in the range of Rs 500 to Rs 20,000 and 36 per cent of them borrowed from NBFCs, 20 per cent of them borrowed from moneylenders, 16 per cent from relatives and 8 per cent from friends. All salaried workers' category, 100 per cent of the respondents have borrowed in between Rs 500 to Rs 20,000. Whereas 44 per cent of them have borrowed the credit from NBFCs the rest of them have borrowed from others sources i.e., relatives (20%) friends (16%) moneylenders (20%). Large size of the family and high dependency ratio have caused them to borrow the credit to maintain their necessities of the family.

Out of the total 281 borrower respondents, 109 of them,

constituting 39 per cent, have borrowed for the consumption expenses, followed by business expenses (35%) house construction and repairs (13%) and the remaining borrowed for religious ceremonies, marriages and for medical expenses. Across the selected categories 84 per cent of petty traders', 48 per cent of vendors' had borrowed mainly for business expenses. On the other hand, majority of the respondents from self-employed, casual labour, domestic labour and salaried workers categories have borrowed the for consumption expenses. Insufficient income from the economic activity in which they engaged might have forced them to borrow for consumption purposes.

In case of savings, out of the total households, 231, constituting 77 per cent of the respondents, have the intention to save, whereas the rest are not able to save any part of their earnings. A majority of them, which constitutes 48 per cent, are saving in between Rs 150 to Rs 300 per month, while 37 per cent of them are able to save upto Rs 150 per month from their earnings, petty traders, vendors, and salaried workers are able to save Rs 150 to Rs 300 per month, whereas self employed, casual labourers and domestic labourers are able to save only below Rs 150 per month and 40 per cent of them from salaried workers' category have no ability to save from their earnings because of their high dependency ratio and large family size, which obstructed their intentions to save.

Regarding consumption pattern, the per capita annual expenditure on food items worked out to Rs 3929, of this expenditure, about 40 per cent is spent on consuming cereals and this is followed by the non-vegetarian items (16%), vegetables (14%), milk (9%) and edible oil (6.50%). Across the selected categories, the per capita annual consumption expenditure is the highest for petty traders (Rs.4390) and lowest for domestic labour (Rs. 3400). With regard to the relative position of different items of the food basket, across the categories, amore or less similar pattern is observed though with varying proportions. The per capita annual expenditure on non-food items worked out to Rs 4154 and it is found to be about 6 per cent higher than the per capita annual expenditure on food items, this expenditure is the highest in petty traders (Rs 6344) and lowest in domestic labour (Rs3383/-). Further, the per capita annual expenditure of Rs 4154/- on non-food items, expenditure on housing, i.e., house rent above constitute about 36 per cent and this is followed by expenditure on fuel (14%) clothing (10%), electricity (10%), education (8%) and entertainment (7%). It is evident that the per capita annual expenditure on addictive items worked out to Rs 328 or less than one rupee per day, about 48 per cent is spent on tobacco and the remaining on liquor. Across different categories, this expenditure is the highest in domestic labour (Rs 486) and the lowest in petty traders (Rs 76). It is also evident, that the relative expenditure on consumption of liquor and social status are inversely related.

The information regarding dwelling type shows that 46 per cent of the respondents are residing in Type II houses followed by 33 per cent staying in Type III houses and 21 per cent residing in Type I houses Across the selected categories, a majority of the respondents from petty traders' are residing in Type III houses, followed by 18 per cent in Type II houses and 16 per cent staying in Type I accommodation. In the vendors' category, 47 per cent of them are staying in Type II houses, followed by 27 per cent in Type I pucca houses and 26 per cent are staying in Type III settlements. While 40 per cent each in the self-employed category are residing in Type III and Type I, the remaining are residing in Type II houses. More than one-half of the respondents from the casual labourers' category are living in Type II houses, followed by 26 per cent residing in Type III and 14 per cent in Type I houses. In the case of domestic labourers' and salaried workers' categories majority of them are staying in Type II dwellings, 51 per cent of the respondents are residing in rented accommodation, whereas 48 per cent of them have own houses. It is to be noted that a majority of the respondents from the vendor's category have own houses (constituting 74 per cent) followed by salaried workers (44%) and petty traders (62%) for the simple reason that they are non-migrants. Out of 64 pucca houses, about 60 per cent are owned and the remaining are rented. Across the selected categories, 88 per cent of petty traders are residing in their own pucca houses followed by vendors (68%), and self- employed (50%). None of the salaried workers are residing in pucca houses. Out of 137 kutcha houses, 51 per cent of the respondents are staying in kutcha rented houses and the remaining are residing in kutcha own houses. As many as 57 respondents are residing in rented houses and 42 are staying in own semi pucca houses.

.Regarding kitchen status 53 per cent of women are using LPG as a main source of fuel for cooking followed by 27 per cent using firewood, 2 per cent using kerosene and 1 per cent using both LPG and kerosene for cooking. Category- wise that 97 per cent of petty traders' 68 per cent of self-employed are using LPG as main fuel for cooking. A majority of them have electrified their houses. Only four per cent in self-employed category, 8 per cent in the domestic labourers' category, three per cent in vendors and 2 per cent in petty traders' categories do not have electricity in their houses. Almost 91 per cent of the respondents have access to protected water supply from public taps, whereas 8 per cent fetch water from public hand pump. Regarding sanitary conditions 59 per cent of them have no lavatory facilities in their settlements and they have to depend on public lavatories, whereas 41 per cent of them have lavatories at their settlements. They depend on public toilets. Whereas, 90 per cent of petty traders, 84 per cent of self-employed, 36 per cent of domestic labour category, 28 per cent of salaried workers have toilet facilities of their own. The settlements do not have separate bathing places and lavatory facilities.

Regarding recreation 44 per cent of the respondents are able to spend in the range of Rs 100 to Rs 150 per month on recreation, whereas, 33 per cent of them are spending below Rs 100 per month. Only vendors, self-employed and salaried workers are able to spend Rs 100 to Rs 150 per month on recreation and rest of them are spending below Rs 100 per month.

In case of health 16 per cent of the respondents are spending Rs 300 to Rs 600 yearly on health and remaining, are scattered unevenly in other ranges of expenditure, seven per cent of respondents are spending above Rs 4000 per year on health alone, that people working in informal sector mostly suffer from nutrition deficiency and poor health resulting from poor sanitation. It shows that 68 per cent of the women respondents are still dependent on husband, father or somebody else only 13 per cent are independent in making discussions and other 19 per cent are not able to say anything. 73 per cent of the women respondents are not participating in welfare organisations. Almost 99 per cent of the respondents are satisfied with their occupations.

7

FACTORS AFFECTING WORK PARTICIPATION RATES AND EARNINGS

In the previous chapter the pattern of investment, borrowings, savings, income and consumption levels of the selected sample households was analysed. Similarly, the work participation rates of the selected respondents engaged in different activities was examined in Chapter 4. Keeping this in view an attempt has been made in this chapter to examine the factors effecting the work participation rate and earnings of the selected sample respondents. For sake of convenience this chapter is divided into two sections. Section I analyses the determinants of work participation rates, while Section II presents an analysis of the determinants of earnings of the selected sample respondents.

SECTION I

Determinants of Work Participation Rates

Work participation rates refer to the proportion of workers to the total number of able bodied persons in the reference age group.

In the study the persons in the age group of 15-59 years is used for analysing the determinants of the work participation rates at the household level. In general, three sets of factors may affect the work participation rates, viz., social background, economic level and demographic structure.

Social background determines the values that the household may attach to education, health and also trade-offs between higher household earnings and the status of keeping away from work. Economic level may also affect the work participation rates in the sense that as income increases, there is a tendency to withdraw women and children from labour force. On the other hand demographic factors specifically the size of the household may affect the work participation rates. If the dependents in the households are more it may increase the work participation rate of women to supplement the males' earnings. On the other hand, if the dependent children are more, it may reduce the female work participation rate.

Specification of the Model

The above discussion clearly indicates that different factors will affect the work participation rates. To determine the relative importance of these factors, multiple regression analysis is employed. The basic form of the Model used in the study is as follows:

$$Y = a_0 + a_1X_1 + a_2X_1^2 + a_3X_2 + a_4X_3 + a_5D_1 + a_6D_2 + \mu,$$

Where

Y	=	Participation rate (Proportion of women workers in the total number of workers in the working age group)
X_1	=	Monthly Per capita Income in Rs.
X_2	=	Sex Ratio (Number of females per 1000 males in age group 15-59)
X_3	=	Dependency Ratio (Number of children less than five years of age per female in the age group 15-59)
D_1	=	1, if belongs to forward caste
	=	0, otherwise
D_2	=	1, if belongs to backward caste
	=	0, otherwise
m	=	Error term or Disturbance term

a_0, a_1, a_2 ... a_6 are regression coefficients to be estimated

Participation Rate (Y)

Participation rate is measured by the proportion of women workers to the total number of workers in the working age group (15-59) of the family.

Economic Level (X_1)

Economic level is measured in terms of monthly per capita income of the households. Further, to assess the impact of economic level on work participation rates over a period of time, the square of monthly per capita income (X_1^2) is used.

Number of female in age group 15-59 per 1000 males in the same age group (X_2) is also considered.

Demographic Structure (X_3)

To analyse the impact of demographic structure on the work participation rates, number of children below five years of age per female in the age group of 15-59 is considered. It is hypothesised that presence of children younger in the household may exert a negative influence on the work participation rates of women. In addition, number of females in age group 15-59 per 1000 males in the same age group (X_2) is also considered.

Social Background

The social background variable is captured by using caste dummies D_1 and D_2 and scheduled caste group is considered as the base.

Findings

The results of the estimated regression equations of all the 300 households put together and for different categories of the households are presented in Table 7.1

Total Informal Sector

All the explanatory variables put together explain about 57 per cent of the variation in the dependent variable i.e., women work participation rate. Further, the F-value indicates that the

Table 7.1: Estimated Regression Equations

Dependent variable (Y): Women Work Participation Rate

Category	*No. of Observations*	*Constant*	*Regression Coefficient of*						R^2	*F-value*
			X_1	X^2_1	X_2	X_3	D_1	D_2		
Over all	300	0.062	0.046 (4.82)	-0.002 (2.11)	-0.0052 (1.36)	-0.059 (2.15)	-0.0100 (2.35)	.052 (2.51)	0.57	29.38
Petty traders	50	0.311	0.041 (2.92)	0.0002 (1.46)	-0.0028 (1.04)	-0.048 (1.95)	-0.057 (2.15)	0.055 (2.28)	0.39	24.31
Vendors	125	0.003	0.071 (3.59)	-0.0017 (1.92)	-0.0018 (1.21)	-0.024 (2.42)	-0.0491 (2.51)	0.1012 (3.11)	0.52	25.39
Self employed	25	0.088	0.032 (3.73)	-0.0062 (1.03)	-0.0007 (1.41)	-0.017 (2.05)	-0.0396 (1.39)	0.2127 (2.37)	0.68	36.53
Casual labour	50	0.056	0.063 (2.71)	0.0053 (0.98)	-0.0002 (0.96)	-0.031 (2.64)	-0.0092 (1.18)	0.2383 (2.66)	0.76	47.31
Domestic labour	25	0.153	0.067 (2.70)	0.0033 (1.79)	-0.0079 (1.20)	-0.035 (2.11)	-0.0138 (1.14)	0.1384 (3.14)	0.71	4089
Salaried workers	25	0.701	0.074 (2.75)	0.0067 (2.18)	-0.0019 (1.58)	-0.042 (2.19)	-0.099 (1.86)	0.094 (2.85)	0.51	33.19

(Figures in parentheses indicate t-values).

co-efficient of multiple determination is significant at one per cent probability level. All the co-efficients have registered the expected signs with *a priori* economic logic. Most of the co-efficients are found to be significant at probability levels ranging from one to ten per cent. The results indicated that a one rupee increase in per capita monthly income will increase women's work participation rates by 4.60 per cent. The co-efficient associated with the square of monthly per capita income, is negative and is found to be significant at 10 per cent probability level implying that in the long run,_increase in income may result in a decline in the work participation rates of women. Similarly a one per cent increase in the proportion of female labour may lead to a decline in female work participation rate by 0.50 per cent. However, this co-efficient is not significant even at 10 per cent probability level. On the other hand, an increase in the number of children below five years by one number will lead to a decline in the women work participation rates by about 5.90 per cent. In addition, the co-efficient associated with the social background dummies revealed that the female work participation rate is higher in backward castes, followed by schedule castes and it is the lowest among others. Hence, it may be concluded that at the over all level, earnings of the households and certain socio- demographic characteristics may exert a positive sign of significance and influence the work participation rates of females engaged in the informal sector activities.

This phenomena at the aggregate level may or may not be equally applicable at a disaggregate level i.e., among different categories. In the foregoing pages, the analysis has been extended category-wise.

Petty Traders

In this Category, all the explanatory variables puttogether have explained about 39 per cent of the variation and the co-efficient of multiple determination is found to be significant at one per cent probability level. Most of the co-efficients associated with different explanatory variables have registered the expected signs, but only the co-efficients associated with monthly per capita income and social background variables are found to be significant at probability levels ranging from one to 10 per cent. The results indicate that a one rupee increase in monthly per capita income will increase women work participation rates by about 4.10 per cent. Here also, the work participation rate of women among backward castes is found to be higher compared to others.

Vendors

All the explanatory variables puttogether have explained about 50 per cent of the variation in female work participation rates and the co-efficient of multiple determination is significant at one per cent probability level. All the regression co-efficients associated with different explanatory variables have registered the expected signs and with the expectation of the co-efficient associated with the dependency ratio all the other are found to be significant at probability levels ranging from one to 10 per cent. Here also, the results indicate that a one rupee increase in monthly per capita income will enhance the female work participation rates by about seven per cent and in the long run it may lead to a decline in the female work participation rates by about 1.70 per cent. Further, it is also observed that the female work participation rates are the highest among backward castes followed by schedule castes and the lowest in respect of others.

Self-Employed

The results of the estimated regression equation indicate that all the explanatory variables put together are explained about 68 per cent of the variation in female work participation rates. The co-efficient associated with monthly per capita income is found to be positive and is significant at one per cent probability level indicating that a one rupee increase in monthly per capita income will enhance female work participation rates by about 3.20 per cent. A part from this, only the co-efficient associated with X_3 and caste dummy (D_2) are found to be significant at 10 per cent probability level implying that an increase in the number of children below five years of age by one number will reduce the female work participation rates by about 1.70 per cent. Here also, the work participation rate is found to be the highest among backward castes and the lowest among forward castes.

Casual Labour

In this category, about 76 per cent of the variation in the female work participation rates have been explained by the explanatory variables considered for the analysis. The coefficient of multiple determination is found to be significant at one per cent probability level. Almost all the co-efficients associated with different explanatory variables have registered the expected signs, but only the co-efficients associated with X_1, X_3 and D_2 are found to be significant at five per cent level of significance. The result indicate that a one rupee increase in monthly per capita income will increase the female work participation by about 6.30 per cent and a one number increase in the children below five years of age will reduce the female work participation rates by about 3.10 per cent. Here also, female work participation rate is found to be the highest among the backward castes followed by scheduled castes and it is the lowest among others.

Domestic labour

In this category all the explanatory variables put together are explaining about 71 per cent of the variation in female work participation rates and the co-efficient of multiple determination is found to be significant at one per cent probability level. Almost all the co-efficients associated with different explanatory variables have registered the expected signs, but only the co-efficients associated with X_1, X_3 and D_2 are found to be significant at probability levels ranging form one to 10 per cent. The results indicated that a one rupee increase in monthly per capita income will increase women work participation rates by about 6.70 per cent. Here also, an increase in the number of dependent children by one number will lead to a decline in the female work participation by about 3.50 per cent.

Salaried Workers

In case of salaried workers all the explanatory variables put together have explained about 51 per cent of the variation in female work participation rates and the co-efficient of multiple determination is significant at one per cent probability level. Most of the co-efficients associated with different explanatory variables registered the excepted signs and the co-efficients associated with X_1, X_1^2, X_3 and D_2 are found to be significant either at 10 per cent or at five per cent probability levels. Interestingly, as against the other categories, it is observed that in the long run also an increase in the earnings will increase the female work participation rates by about 6.70 per cent. Perhaps this may be due to the fact that almost all the women respondents in this category are educated and working as sales girls in different establishments and the prospects of getting higher incomes due to work experience might be the reason. Here also, the female work participation rates is found to be the highest in backward castes followed by scheduled castes and the lowest among others.

SECTION II

Determinations of Earnings

The theoretical basis of the human capital earnings function was provided by Mincer[1] and the Model has become familiar in the labour economics literature. Based on this framework Muzumdar[2], Mohan[3] , Murthy[4] etc have adopted human capital earnings function to explain the heterogeneity of the labour market. Keeping this in view, an attempt has been made in this Section to examine the determinants of average labour earnings by the sample households.

The most widely used framework for examining the determinants of earnings is the human capital model. The model emphasises the role of education, experience and ability in determining the productivity of worker *vis-a- vis* their earnings. The basic model is generally stated as follows :

$$Y= f (S,X, A)$$

Where, the earnings (Y) are assumed to be the function of

schooling (S- number of years of education), length of the experience (X), and ability (A). However, it is argued that this simple model has atleast five shortcomings.

(i) First, it is difficult to estimate precisely the ability of different workers. However, it is argued that it may be possible to incorporate this variable by using shift variables, considering four certain background characteristics like origin of family background, skills etc as proxies.[5]

(ii) Secondly, it may be difficult to measure the schooling variable.

The years of education, which is often used conventionally s this variable, undermines difference in the quality of schooling. Different students may respond differently in receiving education from different schools of varying quality. However, it may be possible to incorporate these considerations also by taking several background variables as proxies.

(iii) The third limitation is from the supply side with respect to the measurement of the experience variable. This model treats the experience variable as creating human wealth through on the job training. The problems with the quality of training would be similar to those discussed in respect of education.

(iv) The fourth consideration from the supply side may be the skill level of the worker which is much more important than the years of schooling for those in the informal labour. The worker's skills levels may determine his productivity more than his education level.

There are also certain personal attributes of workers which may affect the productivity of worker more than the simple human capital variables like schooling and experience. The temporariness of migration is one such possible factor.[6] The marital status and large family size are the important factors influencing the workers to show greater commitment and reliability to the job and thereby they earn more than their counterparts.

Lastly, besides these supply-side considerations, there may be certain demand side aspects which are ignored by the simple human capital earnings function. Evidence suggests that labour market has a high probability of segmentation. According to Mazumdar, labour market segmentation may be that "a difference in earnings can be attributed to the 'institutional' factors after we have allowed for variation in measurable human capital factors"[7]. This indicates that there is a shift in the earnings function, after controlling for the human capital variables, depending on the sectoral location of the worker. The other interpretation of segmentation implies differential returns to the human capital variables which may change the slope of the earnings function for different sectors in the labour market. This may be the result of an inevitable valuation in different sectors of the differential requirements of different activities in different sectors. Despite this limitations 'human capital model' is quite robust in explaining individual variations in earnings.[8]

Model Specification

The basic form of the human capital earnings function adopted in this Study is of the following nature:

Y= f (education, experience, ability, productivity, employment characteristics)

An attempt is made here to incorporate the additional considerations discussed in the earlier section. Now an attempt has been made here to capture the ability through certain background variables which may reflect both the quality of education as well as experience. As it is extremely difficult to measure the possible individual variations in ability for the respondents these individual variations have been ignored.

Following Mazumdar[9] (1979) the productivity aspect is captured through skill level and certain personal attributes of the workers. Finally, the employment characteristics are captured through the sectoral frame used in the Study. The sectoral dummies are the shift variables which indicate a possible segmentation on these lines. The earnings function developed incrementally for the entire sample of 300 respondents, adding variable groups one after the other to test for the stability of the elasticties of different variable groups and the possible additional variance due to the incremental addition of other variables. Further, the sample households have been stratified by sectors and type of jobs to investigate into the possibility of differential returns to human capital variables.

The specific variables used in the equation are:

$$\ln (Y)=b_0+b_1X_1+b_2X_2+b_3X3+b_4X_4+b_5X_5+\text{m}$$

Where

Y = Per capita monthly income in Rs.

X_1 = Education variable

X_2 = Experience (No. of years in this activity)

X_3 = Productivity

X_4 = Social background

X_5 = Employment characteristics, (Sectoral Dimensions)

m = Error term or Disturbance term

b_0, b_1, b_2... , regression coefficients to be estimated.

In the analysis, the dependent variable is transformed into natural logarithm to facilitate the computation of elasticties as well as to reduce the variations in it. The variables are explained here under:

Education (X_1)

This was measured in the conventional way in terms of number of years of education completed,

X_1 = Number of years of education

This was taken as 4 for those who had completed lower primary; 7 for those who had completed upper primary; 10 for those who had completed secondary education. (i.e., 10th class) and 15 for those who had completed college education and for the illiterates it was taken as zero.

Experience (X_2)

This variable is also measured in the conventional way. For those without any education, the age at the beginning of work was assumed to be 10. This may be justified as the average age of the worker at starting work was greater than 10 years.

Experience (X_2) = age- education -6

When the illiterate,

Experience = age -10

Productivity (X_3)

For computing this, two variables viz skill dummy and migration dummy, have been tried to capture their probable impact on productivity

(a) Skill Dummy

D_1 = 1, if the worker is skilled

= 0, otherwise

(b) Migrant status dummy

D_2 = 1, if worker is a migrant

= 0, otherwise

Background Variables (X_4)

To capture the effect of workers' social background on the earnings caste dummies were tried.

(a) Caste Dummy

The Scheduled Castes were taken as the base and the following two dummies are used to classify the caste groups

D_3 = 1,if the worker belongs to the Forward Caste group

= 0, otherwise

D_4 = 1, if worker belongs to Backward Caste group.

= 0, otherwise.

Employment Characteristics (X_5)

To capture the employment characteristics, sectoral frame work which was used throughout the study has been adopted, keeping petty traders as the base group.

D_5 = 1, if the worker is vendor

= 0, otherwise

D_6 = 1, if the worker is self-employed

= 0, otherwise

D_7 = 1, if the worker is a casual labour

= 0, otherwise

D_8 = 1, if the worker is a domestic servant

= 0, otherwise

D_9 = if the workers is a salaried worker

= 0, otherwise

Thus, the final equation to be estimated by incorporating different dummy variables is as follows:

$$\text{Ln}\, Y = b_0 + b_1X_1 + b_2X_2 + b_3\, D_1 + b_4D_2 + b_5\, D_3 + b_6D_4 + b_7D_5 + b_8D_6 + b_9D_7 + b_{10}D_8 + b_{11}D_9 + m$$

This equation has been estimated for all the 300 respondents put-together and also for different categories.

Results

The results of the estimated earnings function of the informal sector are presented in Table 7.2. All the explanatory variables considered together have explained 37 per cent of the variation in the earnings. Further, the F-value indicated that the co-efficient of multiple determination is significant at one per cent level of significance. Most of the explanatory variables had registered the expected signs. The co-efficient associated with education is found to be significant indicating that an increase in the schooling by one year will increase the earnings by about five per cent. Similarly, the co-efficient associated with experience is also found to be significant and explaining that one year increase in experience will

Table 7.2: Results of the Estimated Regression Equations

Dependent variable: ln (Y)	*Regression coefficients*	*t-value*
Constant	2.928	
X_1	0.051	2.17
X_2	0.019	2.70
D_1	0.099	3.93
D_2	-0.025	1.82
D_3	-0.013	1.54
D_4	0.061	2.65
D_5	-0.017	1.65
D_6	0.011	1.33
D_7	-0.035	1.29
D_8	-0.091	2.87
D_9	0.003	1.09
R^2	0.37	
F-value	26.16	
No. of observations	300	

Improve the earnings by about two per cent. The co-efficient associated with skills (D_1) variable is also found to be significant indicating that the earnings of the skilled persons are higher by about 10 per cent than that of unskilled persons. The co-efficient associated with migration (D_2) has registered a negative sign and it is not significant even at 10 per cent probability level. It is thus considered that as an indication that the earnings of the non -migrants are slightly higher than those of migrants, which is in conformity with the earlier findings. The co-effieicents associated with social background (D_3 and D_4) indicates that the earnings of the backward caste respondents are significantly higher compared to others. The co-efficient associated with sectoral dummies indicate that the earnings are relatively higher among the respondents of self-employed category followed by salaried workers, petty traders and it was the lowest among domestic labour. This is also in conformity with the earlier findings though with minor variations

The results of the estimated regression equations for each of the selected categories of respondents are presented in Table 7.3. The co-efficient of multiple determination indicates that the explanatory power of the selected model varied between 30 per cent in casual labourers' category and 49 per cent in the self-employed category. In all these categories, the co-efficient of multiple determination is found to be significant at one per cent probability level.

The co-efficent associated with education variable has registered the expected positive sign in all the categories and it is found to be significant either at five per cent or at 10 per cent level. Only the co-efficients associated with this variable in casual labourers' and domestic labourers' categories are not significant even at 10 per cent probability level. The results also indicated that an increase in schooling by one year will increase earnings by about three per cent in case of vendors, five per cent each in the case of petty traders and salaried workers and by about six per cent in case of self-employed categories.

The co-efficient associated with work experience variable is found to be positive in all the categories and significant either at five per cent or 10 per cent level of significance. The results show that an increase of experience by one year will enhance earnings by about 1.90 per cent in case of vendors, 2.50 per cent in case of petty traders, 1.40 per cent in case of self-employed, 4.20 per cent in case of casual labourers and 3.90 per cent in case of salaried workers.

The co-efficient associated with skill dummy is also found to be positive and significant either at five per cent or at 10 per cent level of significance indicating that the earnings of skilled workers are higher compared to unskilled workers in the selected categories. The co-efficient associated with migration variable is found to be negative in all the categories, except self –employed and casual labourers categories wherein it registered

Table 7.3: Results of the Estimated Regression Equations

Dependent variable: ln (Y)

Category	*No. of Observations*	*Constant*	*Regression Coefficient of*						R^2	*F-value*
			X_1	X_{2}	D_1	D_2	D_3	D_4		
Vendors	125	2.971	0.028 (2.24)	0.019 (2.12)	0.134 (2.45)	-0.030 (1.98)	-0.035 (1.59)	0.049 (2.55)	0.41	26.72
Petty traders	50	2.943	0.049 (2.65)	0.025 (2.51)	0.109 (2.06)	-0.031 (2.341)	0.047 (1.81)	0.059 (2.08)	0.31	22.06
Self-employed	25	2.523	0.063 (2.31)	0.014 (2.47)	0.097 (2.35)	0.070 (1.56)	0.233 (2.26)	0.312 (3.23)	0.49	42.71
Casual labour	50	2.877	0.012 (1.39)	0.042 (1.32)	0.048 (2.01)	0.025 (1.82)	-0.041 (1.29)	0.075 (3.47)	0.30	21.93
Domestic labour	25	2.782	0.009 (1.85)	0.017 (2.10)	0.013 (1.93)	-0.051 (1.96)	-0.008 (1.05)	0.065 (2.76)	0.37	15.69
Salaried workers	25	3.061	0.051 (2.50)	0.039 (2.35)	0.033 (2.30)	-0.023 (2.40)	0.039 (1.07)	0.069 (2.41)	0.43	27.14

(Figures in parentheses indicate t-values).

a positive sign. However, this co-efficient in these two categories is found to be not significant even at 10 per cent level of significance. In the other four categories where in it has registered a negative sign, the co-efficients are found to be significant at 10 per cent level significance. This may be considered as a general indication that the incomes of non-migrants are higher than those of migrants. The results also indicate that the earnings of backward caste respondents are significantly higher compared to others

Summary

The pattern of investment, borrowings, savings, income and consumption levels of the selected sample households was analysed. Similarly, the work participation rates of the selected respondents engaged in different activities was examined. The results indicated that a one rupee increase in per capita monthly income will increase women's work participation rates by 4.60 per cent. The co-efficient associated with the square of monthly per capita income, is negative and is found to be significant at 10 per cent probability level implying that in the long run, increase in income may result in a decline in the work participation rates of women. Similarly a one per cent increase in the proportion of female labour may lead to a decline in female work participation rate by 0.50 per cent. However, this co-efficient is not significant even at 10 per cent probability level. On the other hand, an increase in the number of children below five years by one number will lead to a decline in the women work participation rates by about 5.90 per cent. In addition, the co-efficient associated with the social background dummies revealed that the female work participation rate is higher in backward castes, followed by schedule castes and it is the lowest among others. Hence, it may be concluded that at the over all level, earnings of the households and certain socio-demographic characteristics may exert a positive sign of significance and influence the work participation rates of females engaged in the informal sector activities. The co-efficient associated with education is found to be significant indicating that an increase in the schooling by one year will increase the earnings by about five per cent. Similarly, the co-efficient associated with experience is also found to be significant and explaining that one year increase in experience will improve the earnings by about two per cent. The co-efficient associated with skills (D_1) variable is also found to be significant indicating that the earnings of the skilled persons are higher by about 10 per cent than that of unskilled persons. The co-efficient associated with migration (D_2) has registered a negative sign and it is not significant even at 10 per cent probability level. It is thus considered that the earnings of the non -migrants are slightly higher than those of migrants, which is in conformity with the earlier findings. The co-efficients associated with social background (D_3 and D_4) indicate that the earnings of the backward caste respondents are significantly higher compared to others. The results also indicated that an increase in schooling by one year will increase earnings by about three per cent in case of vendors, five per cent each in the case of petty traders and salaried workers and by about six per cent in case of self-employed categories. The results show that an increase of experience by one year will enhance earnings by about 1.90 per cent in case of vendors, 2.50 per cent in case of petty traders, 1.40 per cent in case of self-employed, 4.20 per cent in case of casual labourers and 3.90 per cent in case of salaried workers . This may be considered as a general indication that the incomes of non- migrants are higher than those of migrants. The results also indicate that the earnings of backward caste respondents are significantly higher compared to others.

NOTES

1 Mincer, Jacob (1974): *Schooling, Experience and Earning*. NBER, Newyork,.

2 Mazumdar, D. and Ahmed, M (1978): *Labour Market Segmentation and the Determination of Earnings*. World Bank Staff Working Paper. No 278.

3 Mohan. R.: (1981):*The Determinations of Labour Earnings in Developing Metropolis*, Estimates from Bagota. Kali Columbia, World Bank Staff Working Paper, No .498.

4 Murthy, K.S (1983): *Urban labour in Informal Sector. A Case Study of Visakhapatnam*. Unpublished Ph.D thesis Andhra University Visakhapatnam.

5. Mohan : *op cit.*
6. *Ibid.*
7. Mazumdar, D (1979): Paradigms in the study of Urban Markets in LDC's: A Reassessment in the light of an Empirical Survey in Bombay City. World Bank Staff Working Paper, No.366.
8. Mazumdar and Ahmed: *op cit*

8

CASE STUDIES

This chapter provides the case studies of 16 sample households. A brief presentation of the family background of the selected households, together with the mode of business operations, problems etc is made in the foregoing pages. Two women each pursuing, fish vending, vegetable vending, fruit vending, petty traders, domestic labour, self-employment, casual labour and sales were selected for purposes of Case Studies.

Case Study 1

Mrs. Sarada, a fruit vendor and Relli by caste (SC) is a native of the city. She is an illiterate having two daughters and a son, younger daughter is handicapped and 9 years old while the elder one is of 12 years old, and the son is of 5 years. Her husband deserted her and married another woman. She has to take care of all the household responsibilities as such. To overcome the financial crisis she took up her age old tradition of fruit vending. She started her small establishment in Poorna Market which in the heart of the city. She vends a variety of seasonal fruits such as oranges, mangoes, papaya, sputa, lime etc. At times, she is helped by her elder daughter, who generally takes care of the household activities. She buys fruits early in the morning from a wholesale dealer in the same market on credit basis and vends. However, she earns Rs 100 to Rs. 130 per day on this. At 9.00 pm she returns home which is nearby. The main problem in fruit vending, according to her, is that the fruits generally come in sealed baskets and she is not given a chance to look into them. Sometimes, she gets damaged ones which do not earn her any profit. Regarding her residence she is residing in her former husband's *pucca* house along with her children. She is sending her son to the Government school and has not been able to educate her daughters. Their house was electrified and are using community lavatory. While coming to the assets they have a transistor, cot, kerosene stove and some aluminum and steel vessels. She is possessing 20 grams of gold by way of '*mangalasutra*' and earrings and she is also saving Rs 200 pm besides meeting the family's basic necessities. For her, this amount is quite helpful to buy gold ornaments for her daughter's marriage. She also wants to continue to save money in the form of private chits to get her younger daughter cured. She also borrows from private financiers for her business operations and also diverts some amount for the household purposes. When she was asked about chits and using the amounts in the business, she was of the opinion that if she takes loans from financers she will have to pay them regularly without fail. As there is no possibility of getting a bank loan for this type of business she has to depend on financiers at exorbitant interest rates. As she is an illiterate she cannot go in for any other job and moreover this work is familiar to her. As such, she wants to continue in the same business. She herself makes decisions even in business as well as in the household activities but she is always afraid of her husband who comes once or twice in a year and torchers her to vacate the house which is his forefather's property. For lack of logistical and financial support both from her in-laws and parents she has to bear this brunt.

Caste Study 2

Mrs. Savitri, a vegetable vendor is a 32 years old Yadava by caste and is the wife of Mr. Ramulu. At present she is vending vegetable at China Waltair junction in City. She is an illiterate and circumstances forced her to take up this business. About 10 years ago, her parents have migrated from Srikakulam to the City seeking better employment opportunities. About five years ago she was married to Mr. Ramulu. About 2 years ago her husband developed extra marital relations with another woman and that lead to their separation. She is living with her sole daughter. She chose vegetable vending, as is an easy job.

She procures vegetables from a wholesale dealer in the Poorna Market with the help of her brother. She buys a variety of vegetables worth of Rs 250 per day. Generally she uses public transport but sometimes she uses private auto rickshaw, which erodes her income margin. She earns about Rs 80 to Rs 90 per day net. She is happy as, she need not pay any taxes for the place but sometimes she faces problem with stray cattle, and also harassment from the traffic police. The other problem she generally faces is perishability of vegetables particularly greens. Regarding her residence she is staying in a semi pucca rented house by paying rent of Rs 400 per month with one electric bulb and without any lavatory facilities. Coming to assets she is having consumer durables like radio, clock, cot, chair, aluminum and steel vessels. She is also having a gold mangalasutra weighing 2.5 grams. Recently she became the member of the local DWCRA and saves Rs 30 per month in the Group. Eventhough she is an illiterate she is quite interested in educating her daughter and she is sending her to the Government school. Regarding decision making she herself decides as she is alone. Some times her brother helps her in business. She borrowed Rs 10,000 from her brother for business an expense free of interest and repays the amount every six months. When asked about borrowing, she expressed that in case she borrows from financiers or moneylenders she has to repay the amount which carries high interest and is beyond her capacity.

Case Study 3

This is a success of an illiterate fish vendor. Mrs. Pollamma a native of Visakhapatnam city got married to Mr. Appala Raju. She is one among the five girls to her father. She used to lead a normal life with the minimum basic necessities of life even in her childhood. Though Mr. Raju is good looking his behavior is deceptive. He is an alcoholic and squanders all his income on it. His lungs are affected and died recently leaving her and the two children (one male and one female). She had to start working for the family's maintenance. She has chosen fish vending which is her traditional occupation. Her children are very young. Now her daughter has got married and her son is working in a scooter mechanic shop and earns Rs 1500 per month .He is also got married to Mrs. Swetha who studied upto 7th standard. Recently Mr. Polamma constructed a two -roomed house. They draw protected drinking water from outside and depend on community lavatory facilities. But their house is electrified, with the help of a housing loan of Rs 15,000 provided to them. Now she is repaying that loan. Her daughter-in-law brought a fan, cot, transistor etc and also 33 grams of gold and 55 grams of silver ware. Though she is happy for owning a house and her children are settled that she is lamenting that she could not educate her son. Hence, she wants to contribute to the family her mite till her last breath. She works all days except when she is sick or during festivals days. She purchases fish from the local fishing harbour and brings them in a rickshaw to her establishment in China Waltair Fish Market. She arranges them and sells to get Rs 60 to Rs 90 of profit. On Sundays, she gets higher a margin. When she started her trade her cousin lent her Rs 2000 and with that amount she started her business and gradually she returned that amount and started depending on daily financier, which forces her to repay it promptly for fear of not getting it finance again. She sells fish till 12.30 P.M and returns home takes lunch and again goes to the Harbour at 3.30 P.M and purchases the fish and returns to her shop and at 8.00 P.M she returns home. The entire household activities are performed by her daughter-in-law. There is no entertainment or no relaxation to her in this work. Of late, she started watching T.V serials in her neighbour's house when she finds time. Regarding decision-making in business she is the sole decision maker, she is also involving her son and daughter-in-law also in decision –making to some extent so that they also know the pros and cons of everything, which they have to face later.

Case Study 4

Mrs. Joythi aged 40 belongs to the vysaya community, which is traditionally a trading community. As such, she had taken up a kirana (petty trade) shop. She is a native of the City. She is one among the four children to her parents. Her father had a kirana shop in Shivajipalem. When he died Mrs.

Joythi was of 10 years. The burden of bringing up the family shifted naturally to her mother. Her mother was an illiterate, unskilled and was forced to enter the trading business. She took the trading business and started earning meager incomes to rear up the children. As children grew, her mother got them married. The natural choice in such a case could be cousins, nephews or near relatives. Mrs. Joythi's mother married her to her cousin. Mrs. Joythi gave birth to two girl children. A result of the consanguineous marriage, one of her daughters is deaf and dumb. Though, she wants to send her elder daughter to the deaf and dumb school, high expenses prohibited her to do so, while other one is studying in a Telugu medium Government school. Mrs. Joythi and husband both run the shop even though she is an illiterate. Moreover, this trade is very familiar to her since her childhood. As her husband is a drunkard and spends the money in consuming liquor she sits in the shop for the whole day. She herself goes to the market and purchases the entire provisions from the whole sale dealer. For this purpose occasionally she borrows Rs 10,000 from a private moneylender and repays them weekly. Mrs. Joythi's weekly earnings after expenses and interest vary from Rs 450 to Rs 500. She goes for the weekly market on an auto rickshaw. She need not pay any taxes to the municipality, as she does not do business outside. Mrs. Joythi owns an old house with one room and verandah which she uses for the shop. It is gratifying to note that Mrs. Joythi has taken a housing loan from the Government and constructed a house which she has let out for of Rs 500 pm. She is now repaying the loan. She is acquiring this property with the hope that such a possession will ensure the marriage of her handicapped child, as a dowry. Her prime concern is to save the bleak prospects of her girl children. Even a normal woman is plagued with the social evil of dowry, contemplation of the marriage of a handicapped woman remains a distant prospect. Mrs. Joythi is busy in her business; her elder daughter looks after the household activities. As Mrs. Joythi s' husband cannot undertake any another work as he is an illiterate. In spite of all these things, they maintain the minimum standards of living and acquired assets for their children. She says that her family life is satisfactory. She also takes an active part in decision making in domestic affairs with the help of her brothers who are educated, who give her proper guidance in case of any problem.

Case Study 5

Mrs. Narayanamma 52 years, a domestic labour is a widow and living with her only son Mr. Appa Rao, daughter in law Ms. Ravanama, 27, and with two grand sons at China Waltair. They were the natives of Bobbili and migrated to Visakhapatnam City some three years ago seeking better work opportunities. Mrs.Narayanamma and her daughter-in –law work as maid servants in the nearby apartments. Both of them leave their house at 5.30 A.M and attend to their work and return home at 8.30 A.M and leave again at 3.30 P.M and work till 5.30 P.M. In the meantime they complete their household activities. Both of them work in three houses each and earn nearly Rs 2, 000 per month. Whereas her son Mr.Apparao works as a casual labour and he is a drunkard and is a lethargic. He is also to habituate beating his wife for money for his vices and both the women bear the brunt. At times, he does not even go for work. If he attends to any work and his contribution to the family earnings is to the tune of Rs50/- per day and the rest of his earnings is spent on liquor and gutka. Mrs. Narayanamma eventhough is an illiterate she got her grandsons admitted in a private school nearby and she bears the entire education expenses. Every year in the month of April she borrows Rs10, 000 from one of her relatives to purchase books, shoes, bags and uniforms for her grandchildren. It is gratifying to note that the children are quite intelligent and are getting good scores in the exams and are rank holders. Hence, she intends to contribute to the family budget till her last breath. Regarding dwelling they are residing in a kutcha house with electricity facility and rent free. They leased in that house by paying Rs 30,000/-on the condition that when they vacate it, the house owner has to return their amount without any interest. They are depending on outside sources for protected drinking water and a community lavatory. At present, she is having debt of Rs 30,000 which she has borrowed from local financier on monthly rate of interest for meeting the medical expenses of her son. Coming to the assets position they have a black and white T.V, cot, radio, wooden table and chairs, aluminum and steel vessels and recently she purchased a second hand cycle for her son at a cost of Rs 200. Her daughter-in-law has gold weighing 30 grams and 30 grams of silverware. Regarding decision-making she is the sole decision maker, as she is an elderly woman and is working for the betterment of their life. But, she has intentions to involve her son and daughter- in- law also in decision-making so that they also should know the pros and cons of everything, which they have to face after her death late.

Case Study 6

This is pathetic story of an upper caste woman. Smt. Sarita an upper caste Brahmin lady aged 28 years old married Mr. Anil who is an S.C. He is handsome and Mrs. Sarita married him some four years ago. After one year of her married life she had to live separately he had all vices like woman, wine etc. As she married without the permission of her parents she could not return to her parents as they did not allow her to stay with them. She has a three years old son. She migrated to Visakhapatnam City to her elder sister's house at Shivajipalem. Mrs. Sarita is staying in a single room. Mrs. Sarita when she was as student learnt tailoring which is helping to earn her livelihood now. She is working as a tailor in China Waltair. She attends to the shop at 8.00 A.M and as she is a skilled person she gets wage on piece rate basis and returns home at 8.30 PM. Daily she earns Rs 50 to Rs 60.While returning home she the next day. She expresses that the amount she earns is insufficient for her though she is staying in her sister's house without paying any rent and electricity charges. Further, she has to look after her son and she wants to admit her son in a good school. She wants to leave this work soon and wants to join elsewhere where she gets a better remuneration. Mrs. Sarita seems, is very much worried about herself and her son's future as her husband wanted to take their son's along with him. But Mrs. Sarita is reluctant to leave her child and she is ready to face any consequences and is not willing to never allow her child to stay with her former husband.

Case Study 7

This is a successful story of a Muslim lady who suffered with her husband's vices and could come up later in her life with satisfaction and contentment. Mrs. Fatima Begum who is of about 42 years is a native of Srikakulam. After her husband's death she migrated to Visakhapatnam City some 25 years ago. She has two sons and one daughter. Her husband used to work in a Government undertaking in Srikakulam. She is residing in Shivajipalem in a single room tenement by paying Rs 250 as rent with electricity. When she came to this City she worked as a maid servant in three, four houses and used to lead a peaceful life getting her children educated. Slowly after three years and making friendship with the local people she borrowed Rs 3,000 from her neighbours and purchased a sewing machine, as she was trained in tailoring. With the same occupation her children studied in government schools and colleges Now her child are grown up and one of her sons joined in the army and sends her some money every month. With the financial support from her son and by stitching clothes she saved some amount and got her daughter married to a government employee by giving Rs2, 00000 as a dowry. Her younger son is working in private company. She wants to pursue this work though her children persuade her not to continue the work. Now with the help of her sons she has constructed a two storied building and the ground floor is used for the tailoring shop. Eventhough all her chores are solved she wants to continue her job which has given her sustenance.

Case Study 8

Mrs. Santamma, wife of Sri. Srinivas 35 years old is a casual labour belongs to B.C category. She is living in Peda Waltair. She is one of the two children to her parents. Her elder sister got married to the Mr.Srinivas and gave birth to two sons and a daughter. When the elder son is about 19 years old, she died. Then Mrs. Santamma's parents decided to give her in marriage to Mr. Srinivas and forced her to enter into the life of Mr. Srinivas who was by then 50 years old. He is a tailor. Mrs. Santamma's mother after her father's death is also staying with Mrs. Santamma. As she is 60 years old she cannot do any wage work. She helps Mrs. Santamma in her household work. Though, she wants her children to continue education, her elder son discontinued the studies and is now working in a cloth shop as a sales boy and earns Rs 1500 pm and the youngest child aged 12 is now studying in a government school. They are living in a semi pucca rented house without electricity. They depend on community drinking facilities and lavatory. Her husband earns Rs 150 per day but spends the most part of it on liquor. Mrs. Santamma's daughter -in -law and her mother are looking after the daily household activities. Her earnings were the main source of income for the family till her elder son joined the work. Her daughter-in-law is uneducated and unable to give proper guidance to the family. Mrs.Santamma is worried about her elder son as he may also get addicted to drinking in the long run. Though Mrs. Santamma does not have own children, she is treating her sister's children are her own. She does not get any support from her husband in any of these activities. Regarding the attitude of her husband towards her work, he does not talk of any thing and he does not give any money to her for the maintenance of the house. Coming to the assets, they do not have any fixed assets like house or land. She is having only liquid assets of 10 grams of gold by way of mangalasutra and 50 grams of silver ware. She is possessing consumer durables like aluminum and steel vessels and a bicycle. As she is a member of a local mahilamandal, she got gas connection recently under subsidy. She is of the opinion that it is a costly affair to buy a refill. Still she is striving to continue it. Before her marriage she used to work as a domestic labour for Rs 500 pm. per month besides helping her mother. After the marriage she is working as a casual labour for of Rs 100 per day. The work spot varies depending on the availability of work. But she is lucky as she gets work everyday unless it is rainy. She leaves house at 8.00 A.M and returns home around 7.30 P.M. When she was asked whether she would like to continue in the same work, she expressed her inability as there was no alternative for her as she is illiterate and also her husband is not co-operative. Once, when she slipped in the work spot and got her leg fractured she had to depend on the daily finance to meet both medical and household expenses. It is gratifying to note that since then she has been wise enough in joining a daily chit by paying Rs 10 regularly and wishes to use it according to the priorities in the house. Coming to the decision making she is the only decision maker and nowadays now she is also discussing with her elder son and daughter-in-law.

Case Study 9

Miss. Saroja a 19 years old who studied up to 10th standard, is a sales girl. She is a Brahmin. She is a native of the Visakhapatnam City. She is one among the five children of her parent's three daughters and two sons. After the death of her father she and her mother had to take the family responsibility on their shoulders. Her mother is working as a domestic servant in a nearby apartment and earns nearly Rs 1000 pm. One of her brothers is working in a motor cycle garage and earns Rs 1500 pm. One sister is studying in Government school another one looks after the household activities. Her father suffered with a lung disease and they spent a lot of amount by borrowing from relatives and moneylender, Mrs. Saroja earns Rs 2000 per month. As she lives in Peda Waltair she has to leave her house at 9.00 A.M to catch a bus to reach the Company in Dwrakanagar. At 10.00 A.M the sales executive distributes the sales girls the items for sale and also indicates the places to sell these items. Carrying the entire luggage she has to roam around each and every house to sell the items she returns home at 8.30 PM. She carries a lunch box with her. She need not work on Sundays and on public holidays. She along with her family members is residing in a semi- pucca rented house by paying Rs 350 pm without lavatory facilities. For protected water they have to depend on public taps. When asked about their liabilities position she expressed that they borrowed around Rs 80,000 for her father's medical expenses which she and her mother are repaying it with interest every month. She could not continue her studies but she wants her younger sister to pursue higher education so as to raise their living standards. Regarding assets they have a black and white T.V, radio, cot, plastic chairs, aluminum, steel vessels etc. They are having 30 grams of gold and 20 grams of silverware. Coming to decision making Mrs. Saroja along with her mother, takes all decisions regarding at the household activities.

Case Study 10

This is another story of a young couple which is an inter caste marriage and leading a harmonious life. It is a story of mutual trust and understanding. Mrs. Shamala upper caste Brahmin is 25 years old is one working as a sales woman. She is married to a BC. Her parents did not approve their marriage and abandoned them and her parent's in-law approve their marriage. At present, they are staying in Shivajipalem. Mr. is working as a security person near a beach side apartment and earns Rs 1,500 pm. As Mrs. Shamala is an educated lady, who studied upto Intermediate wants to support her husband in financial matters. She joined as a sales woman with the help of one of her friends who also does the same work. She leaves home at 8.00 AM after completing her household work and reaches office which is in Dwrakanagar. At 10.00 AM the sales executive distributes the work and indicates the places they have to go and at 7.30 P.M she returns home and attends to her household work again. She gets Rs 2,000 per month. She was told at the time of joining the work that if she performs well, her salary will be increased and has the chances of being made permanent. She is really interested in her job and wants to continue it. Her husband is a gentle man without any bad habits. He looks after her well and both have understood each other. They have a feeling that if her parents also agree their marriage they feel happier. They want to save money from night now planning for the future. Mrs. Mohan expressed that her wife is doing well now and is able to work but after pregnancy she has to leave the job. They want to save for their future. Regarding residence they are staying in a rented pucca house by paying Rs 550 PM as rent with bathroom and lavatory facilities but they depend upon municipal tap for protected water supply. While coming to assets they have a cot, radio, fan, chairs, and aluminum and steel vessels and have the idea of purchasing a T.V soon. She is having 20 grams of gold and 10 grams of silverware. As her parents were against their marriage, they did not give her any durable assets. At present, they are working hard without any support from their parents and in future also they want to lead a happy life without any financial or logistical support from their parents.

9

SUMMARY AND CONCLUSIONS OF THE STUDY

Rapid industrialisation with emphasis on heavy industry aimed at increasing employment and thereby levels of living, ultimately resulted into a growing residual sector popularly known as "informal sector". The ILO has been the pioneering agency which has initiated extensive studies on informal sector (IS) in Africa, Latin America and the Asian countries. These studies have reaffirmed that the existence of the information sector is not a transitory phenomenon and that its presence and contribution are acknowledged at all levels of development.

The Urban informal Sector

The concept of IS has developed in the historical context of urbanisation, migration and dualism. Industrialisation of peasant economics led to the process of urbanisation and large scale migration from the countryside, towards cities. But, due to the slow pace of industrialisation, all the migrated labourforce could not be absorbed in the industrial sector. This surplus labour managed to find avenues of self-employment and wage employment in informal ways.

The urban information sector assumes significance in the context of economic reforms relating to the industrial sector, which offers opportunities for further expansion of the informal sector. In India, over the last two decades, the share of the information sector in the total non-farm employment has remained as high as 92 per cent. Sethuraman (1981) estimated that 25 to 30 per cent of urban incomes in India and Latin America originated from the information sector. Studies on information sector can be classified into two categories, viz., macro and micro level studies. Macro level studies have focused on size, structure, growth and contribution of the Informal sector to the overall employment and the GDP of the economy. Micro-level studies have also estimated the size and contribution of the IS at the city level. Issues relating to the socio-economic characteristics, namely, age caste, education, family system, skill, language and work participation, capital size have been dealt.

Women in urban Informal sector

The Informal Sector has acquired great significance over the years as a source of employment and livelihood for an increasing number of people, especially women in both urban/ rural areas of the developing world. The involvement of large numbers of women in the so-called "informal sector" is a result of their low status in society and denial of opportunities in the formal sphere of employment. Participation of women in socio economic activities is a global issue. Women play a very crucial part in the socio- economic activities and have now become an integral part of global market. Women constitute one-half of the segment of population in India. Women are vital and productive workers in India's national economy. Due to inadequate income of the principal earner, incapacity of the bread earner, death of the bread earner forced women to join the workforce. Female labour participation rate in India has been much lower than in other countries. Due to awareness in women and effects of women's liberation movement etc., the female work participation rate has increased recently.

Objective of the Study

The objectives of the Study are:

(a) To analyse the determinants of work participation rates of women in the informal sector.

(b) to examine the impact of migration on income.

(c) to analyse the determinants of income savings and investment pattern and

(d) to analyse the level of living of women in informal sector.

Methodology

To achieve the above objectives, data were collected from a sample of 300 women respondents working in informal sector of Visakhapatnam city. In the first stage important occupations in the informal sector in Visakhapatnam are listed out, which are petty traders, vendors, self-employed (tailors), casual labour, domestic labour and salaried workers, as they constitute important occupation for women. A pre-designed schedule on the aspects under study was prepared. Based on the observations on testing the schedule, the final schedule was revised and canvassed among the selected of 300 women respondents. The technique used for data collection was stratified random sampling method. The entire area is divided into developed and less developed ones and further subdivided into market areas and residential areas, whereas for vegetables vendors and fruit vendors data were collected from markets and *Rythu Bazaars*. Schedule was designed to collect detailed information from these women working in the informal sector. The present Study has been carried out in a systematic way. A brief description of the universe, selection of sample, tools of data collection, preparation of the schedule, tools of data analysis and design of study are presented in the foregoing pages.

Socio-economic Characteristics

The growth and development is based absolutely on the social factors. The Study revealed that among the total workers, Hindus constitute 97 per cent, followed by Christians and Muslims. In salaried workers' and domestic labourers' categories all are Hindus, closely followed by 98 per cent in the casual labourers' category, and it is more than 90 per cent in the vendors', petty traders', self-emplcyed, categories. In almost all the categories a majority of the respondents are from backward castes and they dominant in all categories of workers. S.C's have followed B.C.'s with a major share in salaried workers' category with 28 per cent, The share of O.Cs' is lower with 32 per cent in petty traders' category, 24 per cent in self- employed category 20 per cent in salaried workers', 8 per cent in casual labourers', with about 5 per cent in vendors' categories.

Across the six selected categories as many as 284 (constituting 95 per cent of the total) are married and among them 244 (constituting 81%) are united, while 40 (constituting 14 per cent) are either divorced or widowed. Education develops the potential and helps a person to be creative. Education and growth are inter-related with each other and it is also observed that out of 300 respondents, 204 are illiterates (68%), 17 per cent of them had secondary level of education, followed by 11 per cent with primary level of education. Almost all the workers from salaried workers' category had secondary level education. Regarding communication skills 54 per cent of the respondents from petty traders' category can speak only in Telugu, 78 per cent from vendors' category are able to speak only in Telugu, while, rest of them can speak both in Telugu and Hindi. Further 24 per cent of them from petty traders' category are able to speak only Telugu. Regarding acquisition of skills, only 9 per cent of them are semi skilled and another 6 per cent have under gone any special training. It is quite interesting to note that dependency ratio is higher in salaried workers' category (1.07%), followed by casual labourers (1.06%) and it is more or less similar in vendors' and petty traders' categories, (1.00% each), and quite low in domestic labourers' category (0.66%).

Migration

It has been observed that in petty traders' category 50 per cent of them migrated for seeking work opportunities, 1/3 migrated to have better employment opportunities and the remaining to accompany their families. From the domestic labourers' category, 40 per cent of them migrated for lack of work at their native places, and 28 per cent migrated to clear past debts. In the salaried workers' category 50 per cent of them migrated to accompany their families. In case of vendors 59 per cent of them migrated from within the District. A more of less similar picture emerges from the self employed, casual labourers, domestic labourers.

The average monthly income of the 133 migrant respondents was Rs 2782 and that of the non-migrants was

Rs 3190. Petty traders reported an average monthly income of Rs 3312 for migrants and that of non-migrants was Rs 3464. Self-employed category reported an average monthly income of Rs 2693 for migrants and that of the non-migrants was Rs 3133.In case of casual labourers the figures were Rs 2846 and Rs 2877. For domestic labourers the figures were Rs 2173. Among salaried workers' category the figures were Rs 2963 and Rs 3200. It shows that there is no significant differences between the migrants and non migrants. The preceding analysis, thus, revealed that migration positively influenced incomes of the migrants.

Income, Savings and Consumption Pattern

The Study revealed that in petty traders' category, 18 per cent of them are investing in between Rs 200 and Rs 500 per week for their business dealings, 46 per cent of them are investing in between Rs 500 and Rs 800 and 36 per cent of them are investing between Rs. 800 and Rs. 1200. In case of vendors, 33 per cent of them invested in between Rs. 200 and Rs. 500, 29 per cent of them are investing in between Rs. 500 and Rs. 800, whereas 26 per cent of them between Rs. 800 and Rs. 1200 per week.

Across the sub division of vendors, 54 per cent of vegetable vendors had invested in between Rs 800 and Rs 1200 per week, while 56 per cent of fruit vendors and 46 per cent of petty traders had invested Rs. 500 to Rs. 800 per week. On the other hand, 56 per cent of fish vendors invested Rs. 200 to Rs. 500 per week to operate their business, 20 per cent of fish vendors worked in fish cutting job and their investment is negligible. All the vegetable vendors, 92 of per cent fish vendors, 88 per cent of fruit vendors, almost all petty traders are depending on the NFBCs for their business transactions. While, 24 per cent borrowed these amounts from relatives, 15 per cent from friends and eight per cent from moneylenders. Lack of provision of collateral securities and easy and informal ways of transaction have made the respondents to approach the NFBCs despite high interest rates. The interest rates ranges from 12 per cent to 60 per cent per annum. Out of the 167 respondents who borrowed, 89 constituting 53 per cent have borrowed at an interest rate of 36 per cent, whereas 50 respondents constituting 30 per cent of them have borrowed at an interest rate of 24 per cent. Only 19 respondents have borrowed at an interest rate of 60 per cent. Out of 175 respondents, 44 per cent of them earned in between Rs 201 and Rs 400 per week, 29 per cent earned between Rs 401 and Rs. 600 per week and 19 per cent of them earned between Rs 601 and Rs 800 per week. Only 6 per cent of them were able to earn Rs 801 to Rs. 1000 per week and two per cent earned above Rs 1001 per week. Across the selected categories, 50 per cent of the vegetable vendors are able to earn in the range of Rs 601 to Rs 800 per week, whereas a higher proportion of fruit vendors (40%) and fish vendors (88%) earned between Rs 201 and Rs 400 per week.

It is found that out of the 25self-employed respondents, 44 per cent of them earned Rs 2001 to Rs 3000, 40 per cent of them earned between Rs 3001 and Rs 4000 and the remaining earned in between Rs 1000 and Rs 2000 per month. Almost all the women in this field are either skilled or semi-skilled and earned better than others compared to other unskilled workers.

Women engaged in casual labourers' category are mostly illiterates and unskilled compared to the self-employed and earned quite less than the skilled workers. It is observed that 44 per cent of domestic labourers earned between Rs 300 and Rs 500 per month as they hardly work for 4 to 6 hours per day in one or two houses to supplement their income for the sake of the family. Almost all of them are migrants and illiterates and are settled in the City to seek employment. It is found that 48 per cent of the salaried workers earned between Rs 1301 and Rs 1500 per month, 36 per cent between Rs 901 and Rs 1100 per month, and the remaining are scattered in other ranges of income. They worked in fancy shops, departmental stores, etc as sales girls and work for monthly income to supplement their family incomes. Mostly unmarried girls work as sales girls as they are educated and have the intention to supplement their families in financial matters.

Regarding income range of the other family members

majority of them, constituting 61 per cent, earned Rs 1,000 to Rs 2,000 per month, whereas 28 per cent of them earned Rs 2,000 to Rs 3,000 per month, while the remaining are distributed in other ranges. A higher proportion of other family members of petty traders, vendors, casual labourers, and domestic labourers have earned in between Rs 1,000 and Rs 2,000 per month. On the other hand a higher proportion of other family members belonging to self-employed and salaried workers' categories earned Rs 2,000 to Rs 3,000 per month.

The average monthly earnings of the sample respondents and of the other family members are also computed. As many as 123 respondents constituting 41 per cent, are able to earn nearly Rs 2000 to Rs 3000 per month. Of these, a majority of them are from vendors' category, followed by casual labourers' and the domestic labourers' categories and the remaining are from other categories. Similarly, another 119 of them (40 per cent) are in the income range of Rs 3000 to Rs 4000 per month and a majority are from vendors' category, followed by the petty traders', casual labourers' categories and the remaining are unevenly scattered in the other ranges

Out of the total 300 sample respondents the annual income of 60 per cent of respondents in between Rs 25,001 and Rs 40,000, while 21 per cent of them earned in between Rs 40,000 and Rs 50,000 per annum. The remaining are scattered in other ranges of income. It is further observed that a majority of them earned in between Rs 25,001 and Rs 40,000 per annum. This pattern of income distribution among, the respondents indicated that the level of poverty is higher among domestic labourers and it is the lowest among petty traders.

The debt pattern of the respondents was also studied and it is found that about two per cent each of the respondents from the vendors' and casual labourers' categories have borrowed above Rs 80,000. While vendors and petty traders have borrowed exclusively for their business operations, rest of them have borrowed for their domestic needs. Among all categories, about 15 per cent of them have not borrowed any amount and they are continuing their activities pooling own savings. The proportion of non-borrower respondents is found to be relatively higher in domestic labouers category (20%), followed by casual labour (12%) and vendors (8%).

Out of the total 281 borrower respondents, 109 of them, constituting 39 per cent, have borrowed for the consumption expenses, followed by business expenses (35%) house construction and repairs (13%) and the remaining borrowed for religious ceremonies, marriages and for medical expenses. Across the selected categories 84 per cent of petty traders, 48 per cent of vendors had borrowed mainly for business expenses. On the other hand a majority of self-employed, casual labour, domestic labour and salaried workers have borrowed for consumption expenses. Insufficient income from the economic activity in which they engaged might have forced them to borrow for consumption purposes.

In case of savings, out of the total households, 231, constituting 77 per cent have the intention to save, whereas the rest are not able to save any part of their earnings. A majority of them, which constitutes 48 per cent, are saving Rs 150 to Rs 300 per month, while 37 per cent of them are able to save upto Rs 150 per month from their earnings, petty traders, vendors, and salaried workers are able to save Rs 150 to Rs 300/- per month, whereas self employed, casual labourers and domestic labourers are able to save only below Rs 150 per month and 40 per cent of them from salaried workers' category have no ability to save from their earnings because of their high dependency ratio and large family size, which obstructed their intentions to save.

Regarding consumption pattern, the per capita annual expenditure on food items worked out to Rs 3929. Of this expenditure, about 40 per cent is spent on consuming cereals and this is followed by the non-vegetarian items (16 per cent), vegetables (14%), milk (9 per cent) and edible oil (6.50%). Across the selected categories, the per capita annual consumption expenditure is the highest for petty traders (Rs 4390) and the lowest for domestic labour (Rs 3400). With regard to the relative position of different items of the food basket, across the categories, a more or less similar pattern is observed, though with varying proportions. The per capita annual expenditure on non- food items worked out to Rs 4154 and it is found to be about 6 per cent higher than the per capita annual expenditure on food items. This expenditure is the highest in petty traders (Rs 6344) and the lowest in domestic labour (Rs 3383). Further, the per capita annual expenditure of Rs 4154 on non-food items expenditure on housing, i.e., house rent above constitute about 36 per cent and this is followed by expenditure on fuel (14%) clothing (10%), electricity (10 per cent), education (8%) and entertainment (7%). It is evident that the per capita annual expenditure on addictive items worked out to Rs 328 or less than one rupee per day. About 48 per cent is spent on tobacco and the remaining on liquor. Across different categories, this expenditure is the highest in domestic labour (Rs 486) and the lowest for petty traders (Rs 76). It is also evident, that the relative expenditure on consumption of liquor and social status are inversely related.

The information regarding dwelling type shows that 46 per cent of the respondents are residing in Type II houses followed by 33 per cent staying in Type III houses and 21 per cent residing in Type I houses. Across the selected categories, a majority of the respondents from petty traders are residing in Type III houses, followed by 18 per cent in Type II houses and 16 per cent staying in Type I accommodation. In the vendors' category, 47 per cent of them are staying in Type II houses, followed by 27 per cent in Type I *pucca* houses and 26 per cent are staying in Type III settlements. While 40 per cent each in the self-employed category are residing in Type III and Type I, the remaining are residing in Type II houses. More than one half of the respondents from the casual labourers' category are living in Type II houses, followed by 26 per cent residing in Type III and 14 per cent in Type I houses. In the case of domestic labourers and salaried workers majority of them are staying in Type II dwellings. About 51 per cent of the respondents are residing in rented accommodation, whereas 48 per cent of them have own houses. It is to be noted that a majority of the respondents from the vendor category have own houses (constituting 74 per cent) followed by salaried workers (44%) and petty traders (62%) for the simple reason that they are non-migrants.

Regarding kitchen status, 53 per cent of women are using LPG as a main source of fuel for cooking, followed by 27 per cent using firewood, two per cent using kerosene and one per cent using both LPG and kerosene for cooking. Category-wise, 97 per cent of petty traders 68 per cent of self-employed are using LPG as main fuel for cooking. A majority of them have electrified their houses. Only four per cent in the self-employed category, eight per cent in the domestic labourers' category, three per cent in vendors and two per cent in petty traders' categories do not have electricity in their houses. As many as 91 per cent of the respondents have access to protected water supply from public taps whereas, eight per cent fetch water from public hand pumps. Regarding sanitary conditions, 59 per cent of them have no lavatory facilities in their settlements and they have to depend on public lavatories, whereas 41 per cent of them do not have lavatories at their settlements. They depend on public toilets. Whereas, 90 per cent of petty traders, 84 per cent of self-employed, 36 per cent of domestic labour category, 28 per cent of salaried workers have toilet facilities of their own. These settlements do not have separate bathing places and lavatory facilities.

Regarding recreation, 44 per cent of the respondents are able to spend in the range of Rs 100 to Rs 150 per month on recreation, and another 33 per cent are spending below Rs 100 per month. Only vendors, self-employed and salaried workers are able to spend Rs 100 to Rs 150 per month on recreation and rest of them are spending below Rs 100 per month.

In case of health facilities, 16 per cent of the respondents are spending Rs 300 to Rs 600 yearly on health and the remaining, are scattered unevenly in other ranges of expenditure, seven per cent of respondents are spending above Rs 4000 per year on health alone. People working in informal sector mostly suffer from nutrition deficiency and poor health resulting from poor sanitation. It shows that 68 per cent of the respondents are still dependent on husband, father or somebody else and only 13 per cent are independent in making decisions and other 19 per cent are not able to say anything. As much as 73 per cent of the respondents are not participating in welfare organisations. Almost all (99%) of the respondents are satisfied with their occupations.

Factors Affecting Work Participation Rates and Earnings

The pattern of investment, borrowings, savings, income and consumption levels of the selected sample households was analysed. Similarly, the work participation rates of the selected respondents engaged in different activities was examined. The results indicated that a one rupee increase in per capita monthly income will increase women's work participation rates by 4.60 per cent. The co-efficient associated with the square of monthly per capita income, is negative and is found to be significant at 10 per cent probability level implying that in the long run, increase in income may result in a decline in the work participation rates of women. Similarly a one per cent increase in the proportion of female labour may lead to a decline in female work participation rate by 0.50 per cent. However, this co-efficient is not significant even at 10 per cent probability level. On the other hand, an increase in the number of children below five years by one number will lead to a decline in the women work participation rates by about 5.90 per cent. In addition, the co-efficient associated with the social background dummies revealed that the female work participation rate is higher in backward castes, followed by schedule castes and it is the lowest among others. Hence, it may be concluded that at the over all level, earnings of the households and certain socio-demographic characteristics may exert a positive sign of significance and influence the work participation rates of females engaged in the informal sector activities. The co-efficient associated with education is found to be significant indicating that an increase in the schooling by one year will increase the earnings by about five per cent. Similarly, the co-efficient associated with experience is also found to be significant and explaining that one year increase in experience will improve the earnings by about two per cent. The co-efficient associated with skills (D_1) variable is also found to be significant indicating that the earnings of the skilled persons are higher by about 10 per cent than that of unskilled persons. The co-efficient associated with migration (D_2) has registered a negative sign and it is not significant even at 10 per cent probability level. It is thus considered that the earnings of the non -migrants are slightly higher than those of migrants, which is in conformity with the earlier findings. The co-efficients associated with social background (D_3 and D_4) indicate that the earnings of the backward caste respondents are significantly higher compared to others. The results also indicated that an increase in schooling by one year will increase earnings by about three per cent in case of vendors, five per cent each in the case of petty traders and salaried workers and by about six per cent in case of self-employed categories. The results show that an increase of experience by one year will enhance earnings by about 1.90 per cent in case of vendors, 2.50 per cent in case of petty traders, 1.40 per cent in case of self-employed, 4.20 per cent in case of casual labourers and 3.90 per cent in case of salaried workers. This may be considered as a general indication that the incomes of non- migrants are higher than those of migrants. The results also indicate that the earnings of backward caste respondents are significantly higher compared to others.

Policy Implications

In the light of the preceding analysis, the following measures are suggested for improving the functioning of women in the urban informal sector and to achieve better results in general and for the proper use of female labourforce in particular.

1. In the ongoing market economy, opening up of markets would make the input and product markets more competitive, and places the informal sector participants in a vulnerable position. Therefore, to improve these informal sector participants restructuring of financial institutions for micro business, improvement of infrastructure facilities and establishment of marketing channels are needed. There is every need for decentralised and need -based promotional policies for their growth and sustainability.

2. Persons involved in the informal sector should be given due recognition. Right type of policies should be developed to ensure that the contributions of informal sector become

more prononounced and people working in it are extended logistical support with sound, commercial, monetary, fiscal, industrial, agricultural and services sector policies to achieve the desired goals.

3. It is the responsibility of the government to create environmental conditions suited for the growth and development of the informal sector.
4. Women working in the informal sector have the initiative. They have the enthusiasm, energy and risk-bearing capacity. The only thing they are lacking in them is skills. They are mostly illiterate. They need training in technology, and need financial support and sound managerial techniques to demonstrate their vibrant success. If these suggestions are implemented, social progress will be accelerated, and their standard of living will improve as time elapses.
5. Credit availability from local banks' branches, marketing linkages, and development of common facility centers may ensure the development of informal sector.
6. In view of privatisation of health care (corporate sector), there is a strong need for health insurances for families of these working poor.
7. Special provisions of credit with concessional interest rates without collaterals should be provided to these women.
8. Government should provide subsidy in transportation costs and abolish several taxes, so that these women can earn more income to ensure higher levels of living.
9. Women in urban informal sector are showing low interest in joining welfare organisations because of lack of time and awareness. It is the responsibility of the welfare organisations to insist these women to participate in them by informing and explaining these women about the benefits, credit facilities with low rates of interest and empower them.
10. If financial, infrastructural, and marketing facilities are given at the right time and place, these self-employed women may become highly enterprising.

11. Another major problem is availability of raw materials, a part from lack of common work-shed, irregular and erratic marketing facilities. They need to be solved for a steady growth and successful functioning of this unorganised sector.
12. A common work- shed in the market places should be provided for these women to keep their products safely and to perform the work, which automatically raises their competitive spirit ultimately.
13. To improve the economic status of these women and to bring them into the mainstream of national development, a combination of multiple policy strategies is to be adopted, such as boosting of productivity and raising of income levels in women's jobs and mobilisation of women into participatory organisations.
14. These women should be helped to get into non-traditional activities also through provision of credit facilities and develop their entrepreneurial skills.

Issues for Further Research

1. Eventhough the informal sector is generating jobs and incomes for the urban poor, with meagre capital investment, the quality of employment still needs to be improved. Working conditions have remained unchanged for many workers, with no fixed working hours. This is particularly true for domestic workers. Studies may be undertaken to examine the ways and means for improving the working conditions of these women
2. Women workers with many disabilities and child workers in particular, need to be targeted. Studies on slum up-gradation and provision of basic infrastructure and services as a successful strategy for simultaneously improving working conditions and productivity levels are to be planned in a more rigorous way.
3. Further most important is about social protection. Informal sector workers need social protection. Therefore local initiatives need to be encouraged and supported through evaluation studies.

4. Involvement of SHGs, cooperatives, local government, workers' and employees' organisations and NGOs is essential in devising appropriate strategies. With strengthened capabilities, they can also help implement support programmes for the informal sector.

   Feasibility studies may be undertaken in a more systematic way.

5. By understanding the problems faced by the informal sector, local government should take initiatives for inspiring a real change within the sector. The urban poverty programmes need to address the problems faced by these informal sector operators. Evaluation studies need to be taken up to provide the ways and means to facilitate easy access to basic services, skills development etc.

SELECTED BIBLIOGRAPHY

Andrea M. Singh "Women In The Urban Unorganised Sector: Domestic Workers, Construction Workers and vendors", *Paper presented at Seminar On "Sex Determination in Gainful Employment*", Indian Institute of Education, Pune, 1981.

Aripse, L "Women In the Informal Labour Sector: The case of Mexico City" in Wellesley Committee (ed), *Women and National Development: The Complexities of Change*, Universities of Chicago Press, 1978.

Aryee, G.A "Education and Training and Informal Sector Employment in Kumasi, Ghana", In: Damachi U.G. and Diegomaon V.P (Eds), *Development*, New York, Praeger, 1978.

Albert, O. Hirsch Man *The strategy of Economic Development*, New Heaven, Yale University Press, 1958.

Aziz, Abdul *Urban Poor and Urban Informal Labour Sector*, New Delhi, Ashih Publishing House, 1984.

Baig, Tara Ali "Women of India-National council of Women in India", *Ministry of Information and Broadcasting*, Government of India New Delhi, 1958.

Bandhopadhyay, Bela "Women Workers in the Informal Sector of Industry In Kolkotta" *Journal Of All India Women's Association*, September 1979.

Bardhan, P.K. "The Political economy of Development. In India" Oxford University Press, New Delhi, 1984.

Basu,D.N. and Sundaram, "The Urban Informal sector: A Search forThe Process and appropriate Strategies" In: Amin,S.(Ed) *Resource, Employment and Development.*, Vol.5 Developing Countries, London, MacMillan.

Beget, Van Den "Entrepreneur Patterns in the urban Informal Sector - The Case of tribal Entrepreneurs in Ranchi", In: De Souza. Alfred(Ed) *The Indian City; Poverty, Ecology and Urban Development*, New Delhi, 1978.

Banerjee, Biswajit *Rural to urban Migration and Urban labour- A Case Study of Delhi*, Bombay, Himalaya Publishing House, 1986.

Banerjee, Nirmala "Women Workers in the Unorganised Sector The Calcutta Experience", Hyderabad, Sangam Books, 1985.

Banerjee, N "The Unorganised sector And The Planners", in K.Bagchi (Ed) *Economy, Polity and Society,* New Delhi, Oxford University Press, 1988.

Banerjee, N "Making a living In a Calcutta", in J. Racine (Ed), *Employment in an Informal Sector*, Calcutta, 1981, New Delhi.

Banerjee (1981) "Rural Urban Migration and Family ties: An Analysis of Family Considerations in Migration Behavior in India", *Oxford Bulletin of Economics and Statistics*, Vol.43, No.4. Page No: 321-355.

Bienfield M. "The Informal sector and Peripheral Capitalisms: The Case of Tanzania", *Institute of Development Bulletin* Vol.6.

Jose, A.V (Ed) *Limited Options – Women Workers in rural India*, Geneva, ILO Publications, 1989.

Joyce, Liebra, Joy Paul Son, Jan Evert (Eds) *Women and Work in India Continuity and Change*, New Delhi, Promilla and Co, Publishers, 1984.

Kamble, K.D. *Migrants in Indian Metropolis: A Study of Madras Metropolis*, New Delhi, Uppal Publishing House, 1982.

Kannappan, Subbaiah "Studies on Urban Labour Market Behaviour in Developing Areas", Geneva, *International Institute of Labour Studies*, 1977.

Karlekar, Malavika "*Poverty and Women Work: A Study of Sweeper Women in Delhi*", New Delhi, *Vikas*,1982.

Kennth, Kamneyer *Population Studies, Selected Essays and Research*, Chicago, 1975.

Kabra, K.N. "Urban Poverty, Un organised Sector and Self Employment Programmes for urban Poor in Development" In: *Programmes for Urban Poor* (Ed) by Girish K.M and K.M Naryan Centre for Urban studies in Indian Institute of Public Administration, New Delhi, 1989.

Kamble, K.B. *Migrants in Indian Metropolis: A Study of Madras Metropolis*, New Delhi, Uppal Publishing House, 1982.

Kelsell, R.K. Pooe, A. *The Graduates: The Sociology of An Elite*, London, Methuen & Co .Ltd., 1972.

Mahajen, V.S *Woman's Contribution to Indian Economic and Social Development*, New Delhi, Deep Publications, 1989.

Mathur, R. N. *Quality of Working life of women construction workers*, New Delhi, Common Wealth Publishers, 1989.

Mazumdar, Atreyi *In Migration and Informal Sector: A Case Study of Urban Delhi*, New Delhi, Vision Books, 1980.

Mazumdar, D.N. *Social contours of an Industrial city*, Bombay, Asia Publishing House, 1960.

Mehta, Prathibha *Women Construction workers with particular reference of legal Security and Social justice, A Case Study of Delhi*, Delhi National Institute of Urban Affairs, 1982.

Meir, G.M. *Leading issues in Economic Development*, New York, Oxford University press, 1976.

Milton, Santos *The Shared Spared- The two circuits of Urban Economy and their special repercussions*, London, Methuen, 1975.

Minser, J. *Schooling Experience and Earning*: New York, NBER, 1974.

Murthy,K.S. "Urban Labour in Informal Sector", Delhi, B.R Publishing Corporation, 1986.

Samal, Kishore, C. *Urban Informal Sector: An Exploration of the Informal Sector in a small City of Orissa*, Delhi, Manak Publications Pvt. Ltd, 1990.

Seema, Rani and Achla Malaviya. *Communication and Rural Women*, Manak Publications (P) Ltd, Delhi, 1991.

Sen, Gupta, Padmini, *Women Workers of India*, Bombay, Asia Publishing House, 1960. *Women in India*, New Delhi, Indian Book Company, 1974.

Shobah, V. *Women in unorganised Sector A study of Warangal*, Warangal Kakatiya University,1984

Sinclair, S.W. "Urbanisation and labour markets in Developing Countries", London, ELBS Publication, 1979.

Sinha, G. Pand Ranade, S. NSrivastava,K.C. "Women construction workers", *Report of two Surveys*, New Delhi, Allied Publishers, 1975."*Women Labour in Glass Industry of U.P*", An unpublished Ph.D., Thesis, Agra University, 1960.

Singh, Menfee Andrea and Anitha Kellis *Viltanen in visible hands: Women in home based Production*, New Delhi, Sage Publications, 1987.

Sullerot, E. *Women, Society and Change*, London, World University Library, 1971.

Theador Caplao *The Sociology of work*, Minneapolis, University of Minnesota Press, 1954.

Todaro, P.M. *International Migration and Urban Employment in less Developed Countries*, 1969.

Tripathy, S.N. and Das Soudamini, *Informal Women Labour in India*, New Delhi, Discovery Publishing House (P) Ltd., 1991.

Uprethi, H.C. *Social Organisation of Migrant Group*, Bombay, Himalaya Publishing House, 1981.

Nathan, J.K.N. and Others (ed) *Towards A Sociology of Culture in India*, New Delhi, Prentice hall of India,1965.

Vishwamitter, *Growth and Urban Informal Sector in Developing Economy*, New Delhi, Deep and Deep Publications, 1988.

Ward, B.E. (ed) *Women in the New Asia*, The changing Social Roles of Men and Women in South and South Asia", UNESCO, Paris,1963.

Wignaras, Poona, *Women Poverty and Resources*, Sage Publication, New Delhi /New Benny Park London, 1990.

Watanabe Susumu *Technological Linkage Between Formal and Informal Sectors of Manufacturing Industries*, Geneva, ILO 1978.

Zachariah, K.C. *Migrants in greater Bombay*, Calcutta, Asia Publishing House, 1968.

ARTICLES

Acharya, Sarathi "The Informal Sector in Development Countries: A Macro view Point". *Paper presented in the seminar on Development and Inter Regional Disparities in India*, held in GIDS, Lucknow, March 19-21, 1983.

Andrea, M. Singh "Women in the urban Unorganised sector : Domestic Workers, Construction Workers and Vendors", *Paper Presented at a seminar On Sex Determination in Gainful Employment*, Indian Institute of Education, Pune, January 1981.

Arunachalam, Jaya "Role of Women and Children in Informal Sector: A case study of working women's Forum, Madras", *Paper presented at the National Seminar on Productivity in the Informal sector*, New Delhi, 1985.

Aryee, G.A "Some notes on intensive Growth and labour Productivity in Informal Sector Firms in Kumasi: A Case study", *Regional Development Dialogue*, Volume 5, No 2, Autumn 1984.

Azad, Nandini "The Social context and Micro Economics and Women- Idly Sellers of Madras city", Madras Working Women's Forum, 1983.

Balasubramanian,N.S "Urban employment in Unorganised Sector", *Yojana*, Volume.12, No.10, June1-15 1984.

Banerjee. Biswajit "The Role of the informal Sector in the Migration Process: A Test of Probabilistic Migration models and labour market Segmentation of India", *Oxford Economic Papers* (New Series), Vol. 35, No.3, November 1983.

Banerjee, Nirmala "Why They get a Worse Deal – Report On Unorganised Women Workers in Calcutta", *Manushi*, No. 20, 1984.

Bhargava, Gopal "Informal Sector", Letter to the Editor, *The Economic Times*, Calcutta, January 10, 1981.

Bienefeld, M "The Informal Sector and Women's Oppression", *Institute of Development Studies Bulletin*, Vol.12, No.3, July 1971.

Birkbeck Chris "Self-employment Proletarians in an Informal factory: The Case of Call's Garbage Dump" *World Development*, Vol.6, No.9/10, September/October.1978.

Bose, A.N "Informal Sector: Problems and Prospect" *Nagarlok*, Vol.12, No.2, April-June1980.

Breman Jan "A dualistic labour System? A Critique of the Informal sector Concept", *Economic and Political Weekly*, Vol. XI, No.48, 49, 50; No. 27, December 4, 11,176.

Bromley Ray and Birkbech Chris "Researching Street Occupation of Cali: The Rationale and method of What may would call an Informal Sector Study", *Regional Development Dialogue*, Vol. 5, No.2, Autumn1984.

Carbo Tara and Morrison Hunter "Nairobi's Informal economic Sector", *Ekistics*, 257 August 1975.

Chaudhari, T.D "The Informal Sector: Product of Structural Imbalance", *Business Standard*, Vol.5, 1985.

Das, Gupta, B "Calcutta Informal Sector", *Institute of Development Studies Bulletin*, Vol.5, 1985.

Das Veechibala "Informal Sector in Socialist Economics: A Re-examination of the Relationship of the Informal Sector to Development", *Regional Development Dialogue*, Vol, 5, No.2, Autumn 1984.

Danies, R "The Informal Sector in Rhodesia: How Important"?" *Rhodesia Science News*, Vol.8, No.7, 1974.

Deshpande, Sudha and Deshpande,L.K "Census of 1981 and the Structure of Employment", *Economic and Political Weekly*, Vol .XX, No.22, June1, 1981.

Dhesi, Atur, S and Wadhawa Urvashi "Productivity, Earnings and Employment Potential of Informal Sector – A Case Study of Nangal (Punjab)", *Indian Journal of Industrial Relations*, Vol.29, No.1, July1984.

Dighe, Anita "Women Employment in the Urban Informal sector: Some Critical Issues", *Social Change*, Vol.15, June 1985.

Espen, Mridul "Women Employment in the Unorganised Sector in Kerala", *Paper presented in the Session on Work and Employment—Second National Conference on Women Studies*, Trivandrum, 1984.

Fapohunda,O.J., Lebell Harold and Lagos "Urbanisation and Employment in Developing Countries: The Role of the Informal sector", *Labour and Society*, Vol.5, No.1, January 1980.

Gosh, Balasnisikha "Displacement of the Female in the Indian Labour Force", *Economic and Political Weekly*, No.24, 1984.

Guisinger and Ifran "Pakistan's Informal Sector", *Journal of Development Studies*, Vol.16, No.4, July1980.

Gulati, Leela "Female Work Participation — A Study of Inter State Difference", *Economic and Political Weekly*, Vol.10 (1-2), 1975.

Harry Oshima, T "Labour Force Explosion and Labour Intensive Sector in the Asian Growth", *Economic Development and Cultural Change*, Vol.19, January 1977.

Hart Keith "Informal Income Opportunities and Urban Employment in Ghana", *Journal of Modern African Studies*, London, March1973.

Hilary, Standing and Bandyopadhyaya, Bela "Women are Employment and the Household, Some Findings From Calcutta. *Economic and Political Weekly*, Vol. XX, No.17. *Review of Women Studies* April-27, 1985.

Holfmann. Michael "The Informal Sector in an Intermediate city: A Case in Egypt", *Economic Development and Cultural Change,* Vol. 34, No. 2 January 1986.

House William "Nairobi's Informal Sector: Dynamic Entrepreneurs or surplus labour" *Economic Development and Cultural change*, Vol. 32, No. 2, January 1984.

Kalpagam, U. "Labour in Small Industry: A Case Study of Exports Garments Industry in Madras" *Economic and Political Weekly*, No. 28, 1981.

Kaptan, S.S. "The Income, Wages and Working conditions of Women Workers in Unorganised sector", *Social Welfare*, May 1989.

Khurana Sarita "Industrial Settlements: Informal Sector dominates Delhi Scene", *The Economic Times*, January. 21,1982.

Lessinger Joanna "Caught Between Work and Modesty: The Dilemma of Women Traders in South India", *Paper presented at the Asian Regional Conference on women and the Household*, New Delhi, 1985.

Lewis, W.A. "Economic development with Unlimited Supplies of Labour", *The Manchester School of Economics and Social Studies*, Vol.22, May 1952.

Lubell Harold. "Urban Development and employment in Calcutta", *International Labour Review*, Vol.109. No.1, July –August 1973.

Madeeha Shervani "Why More women Entering Workforce?" *Yojana*, June 1-15, 1983.

Mathur, R.N. and Mathur Anju "Improving the Working and Living Conditions of Migrant Women Construction Workers", *Paper presented at the National Conference on Women Studies*, Bombay, 1981.

Mazumdar, D. "Labour Surplus in Early Industrialisation in the Case of Bombay Textile Industries", *Economic History Review*, August 1973.

Mazumdar,Dand Ahmad, "Labour Market Segmentation and Determination of Earnings" *World Bank Staff Working Paper*, Washington, 1978.

Mazumdar, T. "Parading in the Study of Urban Markets in Less Developed Countries—A Measurement in the Light of an Empirical Survey in Bombay City" *World Bank Staff Working Paper*, Washington DC, No. 366, 1979.

Mazumdar, Vina "Women Workers in Changing Economy", *Yojana*, May, 1975."Women in the Unorganised Sector", *Paper presented at the Seminar on optimum utilization of women power for Development*, New Delhi, 1975.

McGree,T.G "Peasants in the Cities: A Paradox — A most Indigenous Paradox", *Human Organisation*, Vol, XXXVIII, No.2, Summer 1973.

Mehta, Meera "Urban Informal Sector: Concepts, Indian Evidence and Policy Implication", *Economic and Political Weekly*, .Vol, XXIX, No.8, February 28, 1985.

Moni Sarada, K. "Waiting for Hopeful Tomorrow: International Women Year", *Mainstream*, 13(43), 1975.

Naponen Helsi "Organising Women Petty Traders and Home based Producers-A Case study of Working Women's Forum: Indian", *Paper presented at the Asian Regional Conference on Women and the Household*, New Delhi,1985.

Nath, Kamla "Urban Women Workers—A Preliminary Study", *Economic Political Weekly*, September 11, 1965."Women in Service Occupation", *Economic and Political Weekly*, January 7, 1967.

Nihan,George, Denol, Frick, Jondah "The Modern Informal Sector in Lome", *International Labour Review*. Vol. 118, No.5, September – October.1979.

Orden, R. and Broodhurn, N.M. "Working Wives and Marriage happiness" *The American Journal of Sociology*. Vol. 74, 1968-69.

Papola,T.S. "Wage Determination in the Unorganised Sector in Urban Areas" — A Framework for Analysis", *Gujarat Economic Conference Paper*, Gujarat Economic Association, Ahmedabad, 1976.

Pawar, Amarja"Organisation of the Unorganised Domestic Servants in Pune: struggle For better Working Conditions", *Manushi*, No.21, 1984.

Peterson William "A General Typology of Migration", *American Studies Review*, Vol.23, June 1958.

Raju, R.S. and Ratnam, C.S.V. "A perspective on Unorganised Sector in India", *The Indian Journal of Labour Economics*, Vol. XXVII, No.4, January 1985."Informal Sector in Labour markets: A Review of Literature", *Nagarlok* Vol.XVII, No.2 April – June 1985.

Ranis, G. and Fei J.C.H "The Theory of Economic Development", *American Economic Review*, September–March 1961.

Rao,C.S "Need for technology Up gradation in the Informal Sector", *Productivity*, Vol. XXVI, No.3, October- December 1985.

Rao,V. Lakshmana "Informal sector, Way Below Poverty Line" *Business Standard*, Calcutta, June 13, 1986.

Reddy, Atchi, M. "Socio-Economic Conditions of Women construction Workers in Hyderabad", *Paper Presented at the workshop on Women and Work*. Hyderabad, 1985.

Report of Survey Working Class Women and Working Class Families in Bombay", *Economic and Political Weekly*, July 22, 1978.

Roy, Deb Rama "A Note on Statistical of the Unorganised Sector in India", *Paper Presented at the Fifth Database Seminar*, Madras, 1978.

Sadasivam, Bharati and Singh Sunil "Submissive and Cheap Labourforce—Sales Girls in Madras", *Manushi*, No.13, 1982.

Sahoo. B and Nayak.N.K "The Urban Informal sector and the Problems of Unorganised Labour in Orissa", *Paper Presented in AWDI*, Rourkela, February, 1983.

Samal Kishor "Informal sector: Its Role in Urban economy, Services Offered for Petty trading and Transport", *The Economic Times*, Calcutta, October 13 and 14, 1983.

Svithri, T.S. "Structural Change in Female Employment in the Non-Agricultural Sector in South India", *Economic Review*, 21(14), 1976.

Sengupta,P. "Women in Unregulated and Miscellaneous Industries", *Social Welfare*, Vol. (7), 1954.

Sen, Gita and Sen Chiranjib "Women's Domestic Work Economic activity – Results from National Sample Survey", *Economic and Political Weekly*, Vol. XX, No.17,*Review of Women Studies*, April 27,1985.

Shaw, Annapurna, "Linkages of Large Scale, Small Scale and Informal Sector Industries, A Study of Thane – Belapur", *Economic and Political Weekly*, Febuary, 1990.

Souza, P.R and Tokman,V.E The Informal Urban Sector in Latin America", *International Labour Review*, Vol.114, No.3, November – December 1976.

Standing G.and Skdeo, F "Labour Migration and Development in Gayana", *International Labour Review*, November—December, Vol.116, No.3, 1978.

Suryanarayanan,.S.S "Information Base for the Informal Sector", *The Indian journal of Labour Economics* (Special Issue on Informal Sector), vol.41,no.3

Thippiah. P. "Workers in Urban Informal Sector", *Nagarlok*, Vol (7), No.2, April – June, 1985.

Viswakarma, R.K. "Urban Informal Sector: Concepts, Public Policy and Measures", *Nagarlok*, Vol., XXIX, No.2, April – June 1980.

Uppal, J.S. "Informal Sector in Jakarta", *Asian Economic Review*, Vol.30, No.2, August 1988.

Waldorf, Satal ,Telhat and Waldorf William ,H. "Earnings of Self –employed in an Informal sector: A Case Study of Bangkok", *Economic Development and Cultural Change*, Vol.31, No.3, April 1983.

Week, John "Politics for Expanding in Informal Urban sector of Developing Economy", *International Labour Review*, Vol. III, No.1, January 1975.

Werlin,H.H. "The Informal Sector: The Implication of the ILO's Study of Kenya", *Africana Studies Review*, Vol.17, No. 1, April 1974.

Reports

Adelman, Irma and Sherman Robinson. "Income Distribution and development", In: H.Chenery and T.N.Srinivasan (eds), *Handbook of Development Economics*, vol.ii, Amsterdam: Elsevier Science Publishers.B.V(1989)

Ballantine, Jand R.Soligo "Consumption and Earnings Pattern and Income Distribution", *Economic Development and Cultural Change*, Vol. 26 (1992)

Beneria, L "Accounting for Women's Work: The progress of Two Decades", *World Development*,Vol. 20, No. 11.

Bhatt Ela, R *Report of the National Commission on Self Employment women and Women in the Informal Sector*, Shramashakti ,New Delhi,1988

Economic Commission for Asia and Far–East (ECFAE) "Interrelation Between Population and Man Power Problems" *Asia Population Studies Series*, No.7, United Nations, Bankok, 1972.

Government of India: *Census* Census: India, Andhra Pradesh Visakhapatnam, 1991.

Government of India: *Census* Census: India, Andhra Pradesh, Visakhapatnam, 1981.

Government of India: *Census* Indian, Andhra Pradesh, Visakhapatnam, 1961. Census: India, Andhra Pradesh, Visakhapatnam, 1971.

Government of India: Towards Equality: *Report of the Committee on the Status of Women in India*, Ministry of Education and Social Welfare, New Delhi, 1974.

International labour Organisation: *Employment, Income and Equity, A Strategy for Increasing Productive Employment in Kenya*, Geneva, 1972.

Labour Bureau, "Economic and Social Status of Women Workers of India" Ministry of Labour, *Publication No. 15.*

Ministry of labour ,India *Economic and Social Status of Women Workers in India*, Labour Bureau, Simla, 1953.

Ministry of Labour, "National Employment Services, Area Skill Survey Visakhapatnam", Directorate – *Journal of Employment and Training*, New Delhi, 1976.

National Commission on Labour, Ministry of Employment and Rehabilitation, New Delhi, 1969.

Planning Commission, *Draft Five Year Plan, 1978-1983*. New Delhi.

Planning Commission, Government of India, *Eighth Five-year Plan, 1992 –1997*, New Delhi, 1997.

Planning Commission, *Third Five year Plan, 1961-1966*. New Delhi,1961

Report on Workshop on the Unorganised sector, Ahmedabad, SEWA, 1984.

Women in the Urban Informal Sector National Institute of Urban Affairs Research study series, No.49

INDEX

❑❑❑